Develop Your Cybersecurity Career Path

How to Break into Cybersecurity at Any Level

Gary Hayslip, Christophe Foulon, Renee Small

Copyright © 2021 CISO DRG

Develop Your Cybersecurity Career Path
How to Break into Cyber Security at Any Level

ALL RIGHTS RESERVED

No part of this book may be reproduced, stored in a retrieval system, or transmitted in any form, or by any means whether by electronic, mechanical, photocopy, recording or otherwise, without the prior written permission of the copyright owner except in the case of a brief quotation embodied in a critical review and certain other noncommercial uses permitted by copyright law. For all other uses, requests for permission may be sent to the publisher, "Attention: Permissions Coordinator," at the address below:

> CISO DRG Publishing
> P.O. Box 928115
> San Diego, CA 92192
> <www.CISODRG.com>
> info@cisodrg.com
> ISBN 978-1-955976-00-8

DISCLAIMER: The contents of this book and any additional comments are for informational purposes only and are not intended to be a substitute for professional advice. Your reliance on any information provided by the publisher, its affiliates, content providers, members, employees or comment contributors is solely at your own risk. This publication is sold with the understanding that the publisher is not engaged in rendering professional services. If advice or other expert assistance is required, the services of a competent professional person should be sought.

To contact the authors, write the publisher at the address provided above, "Attention: Author Services."

> Edited by Bill Bonney
> Artwork by Gwendolyn Peres
> Formatting by Last Mile Publishing

Dedication

Gary

I would like to dedicate this book to my best friend, and wife of 30 years Sandi Hayslip. She has been with me through my time on active duty and its long deployments keeping our family strong. She is the rock that we gather around and the life friend I have to talk to on long walks. Her insight, strength, and faith have been an example for me to aspire towards and I am grateful that she continues to encourage me to lead and stay engaged in our cyber community.

Chris

I would like to dedicate this book to my wife, Emily, and son, Landon. They have been my rock and support through times of success and struggle. They are the reason I strive to work harder and provide them with the support they deserve. Landon, while I hope to have you follow in my footsteps, I will strive to make this industry a place which is inviting and accepting of all. I am the change I want to see in this world, so that it will be a better place for you.

Renee

I dedicate this book to my husband, Jason, and three children, Justin, Cameron, and Julia. They are my inspiration and support me as I embark on many, many endeavors.

Acknowledgments

The authors would like to acknowledge the following people for their contributions, directly or indirectly, in giving us encouragement, providing resource materials or assistance with proofreading the manuscript, and otherwise giving us the inspiration to write this book.

Gary Hayslip: To my best friend, my wife of 30 years, I would like to say thank you for all of your support and understanding. She has been with me through my time on active duty and its long deployments, keeping our family strong. She is the rock that we gather around and the life friend I have to talk to on long walks. Her insight, strength, and faith have been an example for me to aspire towards and I am grateful that she continues to encourage me to lead and stay engaged in our cyber community.

To my co-authors, this has been an amazing journey and I truly appreciate your hard work, patience, laughter, and insight that has helped me and kept me focused throughout this endeavor.

Finally, to the security community, this book is for you. It is meant to be a guide to help you as you develop and walk your career path and I am truly humbled to be a part of your journey.

Chris Foulon: I would like to thank my wife and son, who patiently support me as I passionately contribute to the cybersecurity community and those who are breaking into cybersecurity through ventures like my podcast (Breaking into Cybersecurity), courses and coaching, and of course this book.

I would also like to thank the cybersecurity community and Security Tinkerers who have been extremely supportive of me throughout the years. I hope that I can continue to pay it forward for years to come.

I really appreciated the process of writing this book, which demonstrates how diversity of thoughts and experiences can lead to the betterment of the cybersecurity community and why it's so critical in the hiring and team-building process as well.

Renee Small: To my husband, Jason, and our three little ones; thank you for your love and support and sometimes being my writing companions in the wee hours of the morning when it was quiet enough to write this book.

To my co-authors Matt and Chris, and our editor, Bill; thank you for your patience, support, and guidance through this book-writing process.

Lastly, to all the podcast guests and audience members, the interviewees, and the many people who reached out about how they have broken into Cybersecurity; thank you for sharing your stories and giving knowledge, hope, and inspiration to the ones coming up behind you.

Table of Contents

Preface i
How to Use This Book iii
Introduction v
The Start of Your Journey 1
   1. Is a Career in Cybersecurity for You? 3
      Introduction 3
      The Questions You Must Ask Yourself - Gary 5
      Just an Island Boy Finding Out About Technology - Chris ... 12
      Anyone Can Have a Career in Cybersecurity - Renee 19
      Key Points and Recommended Actions 25

Self-Assessment 27
   Introduction 29
   2. Where to Begin? 31
      Introduction 31
      My Path to a Career in Cybersecurity - Gary 32
      Finding Your Passion - Chris 44
      What Should Be Your First Steps? - Renee 54
      Key Points and Recommended Actions 60
   3. Taking Inventory 61
      Introduction 61
      Improving Your Technical Skills and Key Resources - Gary 63
      Skills Assessment - Chris 71
      Hiring Managers Also Do Assessments - Renee 79
      Key Points and Recommended Actions 82
   4. Soft Skills 83
      Introduction 83
      Cyber Soft Skills and Then Some - Gary 85
      Don't Forget About the Soft Skills - Chris 88
      Soft Skills in Practice - Renee 91
      Key Points and Recommended Actions 94

Your Human Network 95
   Introduction 97
   5. Your Network and the Cyber Community 99
      Introduction 99

Maturing Your Career Map and Joining Our Community
– A Plan for Success! ~ Gary 101
Why Growing a Network Is Important ~ Chris 110
How to Build a Network that Works for You ~ Renee 117
Key Points and Recommended Actions 122

6. Social Media 123
   Introduction 123
   Mature Your Social Media Footprint ~ Gary 125
   Social Media ~ Chris 129
   Social Media ~ Renee 139
   Key Points and Recommended Actions 144

The Job Search 145
   Introduction 147
   7. Building Your Cyber Résumé 149
      Introduction 149
      Writing a Cybersecurity Résumé ~ Gary 151
      Building and Tailoring Your Résumé for Success ~ Chris ... 159
      The Anatomy of a Cyber Résumé ~ Renee 164
      Key Points and Recommended Actions 170

   8. Searching for a Cybersecurity Job 171
      Introduction 171
      Searching for Your First Cybersecurity Job ~ Gary 173
      Searching for Your Cybersecurity Job ~ Chris 185
      How to Search for a Job ~ Renee 191
      Key Points and Recommended Actions 198

   9. The Cybersecurity Job Interview 199
      Introduction 199
      Preparing for Your Cybersecurity Job Interview ~ Gary ... 201
      The Cybersecurity Interview ~ Chris 209
      The Job Interview ~ Renee 216
      Key Points and Recommended Actions 222

   10. Recruiters and How to Use Them in Your Job Search 223
      Introduction 223
      Working with Recruiters in Cybersecurity – Some Basics
         You Should Know ~ Gary 224
      How Best to Use a Recruiter ~ Chris 229
      The Recruiter's Role ~ Renee 234

Key Points and Recommended Actions 243
The Next Stage of Your Journey 245
   11. Working in Cybersecurity 247
      Introduction 247
      Working in Cybersecurity – Steps for Developing your New
          Cyber Career Plan ~ Gary 248
      You Are Here, Now What? ~ Chris 256
      Congratulations! You Made it! Now What? ~ Renee 264
      Key Points and Recommended Actions 268
Conclusion 269
About the Authors 271

Preface

Gary Hayslip, Christophe Foulon, and Renee Small have very different backgrounds and one essential shared passion. That passion is to help people who wish to join the profession they care so deeply about, Cybersecurity. For Gary, that passion is born of the combination of intense curiosity about technology and a desire to protect and serve. For Chris, a desire to help people learn to safely use the emerging technologies that were allowing people from his native Caribbean home to connect with the rest of the world. And for Renee, the amazing and rewarding challenge of finding all the purple squirrels and superheroes that companies need to protect their networks from the thieves and spies looking to harm them every day.

We've all heard the horror stories. Breach after breach; threats reported against our healthcare system, our government services, and every aspect of our critical infrastructure, seemingly without end. Many are willing to answer the call, but they don't know how to break into the field. The need is real, with unfilled job postings numbering in the millions. As we're fond of saying, enough talking about the problem, what are we going to do about it?

Gary has been writing articles and mentoring would-be cyber-warriors for several years. He has selflessly shared every aspect of his journey, from the head-shaking behavior of clueless recruiters to the vulnerabilities of not feeling qualified for the job that would help him provide for his family when he left the military after a long and secure career. Chris and Renee have been hosting a weekly podcast called Breaking into Cybersecurity since September of 2019, having met just before then online, engaging with the community. The three authors met online, using the same networking techniques they recommend throughout this book.

There is no better way to blend these varied perspectives than to use the tri-perspective storytelling technique that Gary helped pioneer along with Bill Bonney and Matt Stamper, the three amigos that authored the CISO Desk Reference Guide and now publish the CISO DRG catalog of titles. Gary, Christophe, and Renee care deeply about their chosen career field and our collective mission. In addition to shepherding their own careers, each has been involved in hiring, developing, and mentoring cyber-pros and would-be cyber-pros for years. In *Develop Your Cybersecurity Career Path*, they each share their perspective about the career, the community, and the commitment and how you can develop your cybersecurity career and land your first cybersecurity job.

How to Use This Book

The order of the essays within each chapter follows the arc of the authors' differing backgrounds and perspectives. Gary Hayslip's essays lead off each chapter and provide a high-level view reflecting his background as a technologist, cyber-warrior, and now a Chief Information Security Officer (CISO). He shares what he has learned, having built teams and programs, developed staff, mentored colleagues, and worked with the greater cybersecurity community. Christophe Foulon's essays come next, and his perspective on providing services to customers, as well as the self-taught knowledge he acquired, includes insight from the trenches. Finally, Renee Small's essays finish each chapter. Her experience as both a cybersecurity professional and a recruiter provides the reader with the inside scoop on navigating the daunting world of screening and interviewing.

It may be tempting as you start to get familiar with the writers' styles to skip ahead and read the next essay by your favorite author. We caution you to resist that as much as you can. Readers have shared that triangulating the essay topics from three perspectives, sometimes closely aligned and sometimes highlighting very different points, is invaluable. Especially when you are just starting out on your cybersecurity journey, each additional perspective can give you the leg up you need. Later, as you are comfortable in your new job and working on your career path, you might take the approach of following one particular author's arc. Even so, don't neglect the other two – each has carved out a successful path, and there is something to learn from each essay.

At times we're going to recommend that you print out your résumé and mark it up or get out a piece of paper or a notebook and roll up your sleeves. This is an action-oriented book. There are 60 key points and recommended next steps. While there is no requirement to follow every recommendation at the end of every chapter, if you are wondering "now what," we've got you covered. There is nothing passive about cybersecurity. It is a full-contact team sport.

Introduction

Any course in macroeconomics will talk about the forces acting upon the economy to keep supply and demand in a state of equilibrium. Whether the discussion is about goods or services and labor, when the demand goes up, the theory goes, buyers are willing to pay more, and the supply should then follow. But one of the constant qualifiers when teaching about this system of economics is: "all other things being equal." When it comes to the cybersecurity workforce, the demand signal has gone out, but all things are not equal.

Put plainly, there is a labor (supply) shortage in the cybersecurity field, and prices (wages) have gone up, but we are still woefully understaffed. Why? Has the theory of supply and demand been disproved? In our opinion, not at all. What is unequal, at the moment, is the number of candidates who are or think they are qualified for a career in cybersecurity.

For those that want to explore a career in cybersecurity, we first want to say, "Welcome, we need the help!" Cybersecurity is a career dedicated to a mission to protect. At the same time, it is very rewarding—both in knowing that what you do makes a difference and, frankly, unmatched job security. Unfortunately, the cybersecurity field has many more positions available than qualified candidates.

In the pages that follow, we'll show you how to break into cybersecurity at any level. Whether you are just starting out and are looking for an entry-level position or want to translate many years of experience to a job in cybersecurity at the right level, this book will help. We have organized the book into five sections. We start in Section One with the beginning of your journey and help you determine if this is the right field for you. In Section Two we give you the tools to conduct a self-assessment to see how you stack up to the requirements of the field and what you need to do to close any gaps.

After the self-assessment, we transition in Section Three to your human network and show you how to build a personal network and capitalize on your network to help you with your job search. Then, in Section Four, we move on to the job search itself. This section covers the résumé, job search, interviewing, and how to use recruiters in your search. Finally, in Section Five, we provide you with some sage advice as you transition into your cybersecurity career.

Each chapter consists of five parts. First, there is an introduction that sets up the topic for that chapter. Then each of the three authors provides their unique perspectives on the subject. Each chapter concludes with key points and actions.

Throughout the book, we've footnoted both supporting references and resources that we have found helpful. At the end of Renee's sections, there are additional sets of resources.

A career in cybersecurity is both demanding and rewarding. We welcome you on your journey and are excited to share what we have learned so you can join the team all the sooner.

Section 1

The Start of Your Journey

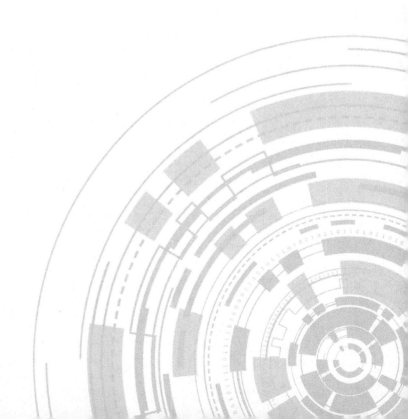

Chapter 1

Is a Career in Cybersecurity for You?

Introduction

The basic definition of cybersecurity is the practice of protecting systems, networks, and programs from digital attacks. Individuals and enterprises use the practice to protect against unauthorized access to data centers, digital assets, and other computerized systems. That sounds relatively simple, but as we're sure you know, nothing in cybersecurity is simple. From the outside looking in, the field appears vast and highly technical. Cybersecurity seems to be continuously changing, and workers in this field are in high demand by companies worldwide. That leads to the question we know many of you are asking yourselves: "Is this type of job for me?" Followed by the next question we know you've been pondering and want an answer to: "How do I go about finding a job in cybersecurity?" Well, we are here to help you with those questions.

In this first chapter, we discuss our viewpoints about working in cybersecurity and try to provide you with the essential information you need to answer the question of whether working in cybersecurity is for you or not. All three of us come from amazingly diverse backgrounds and found our way into this career field by following different paths. However, as you read this chapter, you will note there are core principles that all three of us agree on about working in cybersecurity.

So, we invite you to enjoy these three essays. Approach this with an open mind. You'll see the passion we have for our chosen careers and the community of professionals which we are proud to be a part of.

We know this field may not be suitable for everyone; it will require you to work to find your path, and because of the very dynamic nature of the job field, you will have to educate yourself and stay current continuously. However, don't feel daunted because that's why we are here, providing you with the essential tools that you will need to be successful if you want to join our community.

At the end of the chapter, we summarize some key takeaways and provide a short list of next steps to get your started.

With that said, dive into Chapter 1, and see if cybersecurity is right for you!

The Questions You Must Ask Yourself ~ Gary

I recently spent an afternoon volunteering to work at a job fair and discuss my career in cybersecurity. At this fair were many students from local high schools, junior colleges, and four-year universities, and many veterans transitioning into civilian life. As the afternoon wore on I fielded numerous questions. I found many of the questions interesting and decided to write them down. I realized later that evening that these were questions that I had asked myself years ago when I started my career. I thought I would share the top nine questions and my answers to them.

1. What cybersecurity career options are there?

Cybersecurity isn't a career field with only one or two options. Even after working in this field for over 15 years, I find that it is continually evolving. The definition of cybersecurity is the use of preventative techniques and methodologies to protect the integrity of networks, programs, and data from attack, damage, or unauthorized access. As you can imagine, that is quite broad. I tell my executive staff that cyber, in many ways, is like water that flows throughout the organization into every division, department, and operational program. In essence, no matter what business unit or department you work in, you will use technology to do your job. There will be rules, policies, security technology, and security controls deployed to ensure you can use that technology and the data you create effectively but securely.

Your options are, therefore, pretty broad. There are entry-level positions such as technicians and analysts, and engineers and architects who work on the more significant aspects of security programs and teams. There are program managers, directors, and executives (CISO, CSO) who manage security projects, programs, departments, and multiple teams. There are also sales engineers (selling security products), security consultants, and advisors who help organizations implement new security technologies and advise and assist leadership in setting security planning and long-term strategy. This career field is maturing. Numerous jobs are open with job descriptions that can change quickly depending on the business' needs, technology changes, or new threats. My answer is, therefore, that there are many options open to you. You will find over time that in this field you can move around and try new positions until you find one that feels right for you.

2. How would I stay up to date in this field?

I get asked this question by many people interested in a career in cybersecurity. Unfortunately, if you are looking for a job where you can know everything, this is not the career for you. I've been in the IT field and cybersecurity field for a combined 20+ years, and I find I am continually learning new things. If you plan to work in this field, I recommend you get comfortable with continuous learning. First, you need to get into a routine of reading articles, magazines, blogs, and other sources to stay up with what is happening in the technology field. As changes occur in technology, there will be residual impacts in cybersecurity and vice versa.

After you get your reading schedule set up, I suggest you look at professional organizations to join. This networking activity allows you to gather with peers, and at the meetings you can enjoy presentations on topics of interest. I would then look at classes at local colleges. You can take courses on interesting subjects that pertain to some new technology, programming language, or security methodology. My final suggestion is to look at possible online classes, select a topic to learn about or a certification that you want to pursue. All of these suggestions are methods I continuously use to keep up. Even as a CISO, I am still attending classes and working on certifications. I find the challenge rewarding, and I feel it's essential for me to understand the emerging challenges in my field.

3. Is there a technology I should learn first?

I would first look at what is my baseline knowledge of working with computers. Most people have some limited experience with computers, tablets, smartphones, or wearables. If you don't have very much, I would suggest you take an introductory class on computers and then a course on networks. Having a working knowledge of networks is invaluable in cybersecurity. After these two areas, I would advise you to take a programming class to get comfortable with writing code. I have my security engineers learn Python, so they are comfortable with writing scripts when needed.

After you have completed these basics, you can focus on what you liked from the classes you took. If you liked writing code, then I would look at software development as a field of interest. There is significant research underway on how to implement "security by design" or DevSecOps. DevSecOps involves writing code with security as part of the development life cycle.

If you enjoyed the course on networks, I would recommend you investigate becoming a network architect. As you move into that specialty, focus on learning more about network security. Another option, if you decide you like networking and you want to learn about how to build virtual networks, is to look at taking classes on Amazon Web Services (AWS) or Azure.

I am currently working on AWS certifications. I have seen many of the security services I use offered in cloud variants, so I am getting cloud certified. Studying for these certifications will allow me to understand how to implement and protect these services.

If you complete the basic classes and still aren't sure what to do next, consider becoming involved in IT/Cyber professional organizations. Ask for advice. Many of us are willing to help you weigh the pros and cons. We need good people in our community, and we are here to help.

4. Will cybersecurity be a relevant career field for me in the future?

I have fun with this question. It is typically centered on discussions that Artificial Intelligence (AI) is going to replace every cybersecurity process. Now I do believe machine learning and other forms of AI will become more prevalent in this field. However, I do not think they will replace the need for humans to work in this field. In fact, I want to use these technologies to automate many of the processes I have and find ways to integrate my security stack so my technologies can share information and my team, and I can make better-informed decisions in real time. Note, I said we (humans) are making the decisions, which means that yes, I wholeheartedly believe this career field will be here long term. Now with that said, I do want to point out it is a field that is in a constant state of flux because we are linked with changes in technology. As there are recent technology advances, you will see this field accelerate, so again this field will be here in the future, but it will be changing, so you will need to stay active to be relevant in your position.

5. How would I get experience in this field?

I get this question from many veterans who are transitioning. Being prior military myself, I know we are trained to see an objective and break it down into achievable components and then get to work. I like to refer to how I did it myself and use my career as an example. I explain to many veterans that going to school for a degree in cybersecurity gets you a degree, but you still need the experience to go with that degree. I suggest that many of them first get involved with professional organizations such as ISACA, ISC2, ISSA, OWASP, AITP, IAAP, and InfraGard. Getting involved with these organizations allows you to network with peers in your area and find out about any available entry-level positions or intern positions that may be available. I then suggest they look at non-profits in their area. I provided IT services for several non-profits over the two years I took to complete my network certifications. It allowed me to put on my résumé that I was providing critical services to an organization. I also had the opportunity to put into practice what I was learning from my classes and while studying for my certifications.

Just understand that many people working in the cybersecurity community came from other professions, and many of us started in entry-level positions such as network administrators, helpdesk support technicians, and quality assurance specialists. You will probably be in one of these entry-level positions and must work your way up, even with a degree. Don't lose faith. Stay focused on the objective and cyber up. Keep pushing forward, select various positions with greater responsibility over time and keep adding to your education, so you are ready when opportunity knocks.

6. Will this field be boring?

This question always makes me laugh. I wish, or better yet, no, I don't, because I like organized chaos. No, this field is not boring. Now understand that you may have a position where you feel like you are in cubicle prison and you have one task that you do repetitively day in and day out. Therefore, get involved with the professional organizations in your community, build your network, and continuously educate yourself. If you find yourself bored in your job and feel that it's time to move on, you will have the resources to do it. That is one thing about this field. There are so many different aspects that apply to cybersecurity that you can move around and find a position that engages you, so don't accept sitting in a cubicle if you want to make a change. Instead, find a job that fills your needs, assess what is required to qualify for it, and when you are ready to make the jump, please do it. We need you in our community.

7. What do you like about your career in cyber and why should I pursue one?

I like that my career in cybersecurity is challenging, and in many ways, I always feel like I have so much to learn. I love giving back to the community and mentoring new CISOs and veterans transitioning into this field. I am also fascinated with technology and all the interesting and scary ways to deploy it. I have been a CIO, Deputy CIO, Network Architect, and CISO. In all those positions, I have genuinely enjoyed the challenge of managing large-scale technology infrastructures, programs, departments, and the risks involved with operating them. I feel blessed to be given the opportunity to mentor teams and have the good fortune to work with organizations on the cutting edge of new technologies. What I would say to people coming into this field now is that your experience will be vastly different from mine. Changes in Information Technology will continue to accelerate, and our cyber defenses will need to continue to evolve and scale to meet emerging threats. With that in mind, you will have opportunities to work with various new technologies across myriad deployment models for organizations that will desperately need your services. And you will have the ability to grow your capabilities exponentially with these technologies. I think a career in this field will be challenging for you, but it will be one that you can continuously excel at if you want to put the time and effort into it.

8. I like to help people. How would working in this field serve others?

Cybersecurity is dynamic and evolves as new technologies such as IoT, cloud, SDN, and block-chain become commonplace. As these technologies grow in use, security grows with them because there will always be cyber-criminal elements that will look to exploit new technologies. That is where the field of cybersecurity provides value. I know many people who join this field because they came from a career of service, and in cybersecurity, they can still enjoy being part of a team and providing value to an organization. Now obviously, this doesn't equate to working for an organization that directly helps the homeless or provides aid to those stricken by a natural disaster. But, in both cases, the teams in the field will need technology to provide services, and the unfortunate reality is that cyber-criminals tend to prey on the chaos. Security technologies safeguard the supply chain that provides needed supplies, protects sensitive data collected from those who need assistance, and secures communications channels between workers in the field and their organization. These are just a few examples of how working in cybersecurity can provide service to others. People in this community continually offer free services to non-profits and have donated their spare time to assist charities in setting up and securing their networks. Yes, you can serve others by working in this field, and there are infinite ways to do it.

9. I may want to travel. How portable is a job in this field?

Because of the breadth of technology and how every continent is connected to the global Internet, the answer to this question is yes, your job is portable. There are some caveats to that. Some countries require different training or certifications, and some industries may differ in requirements depending on where you are located. For example, the data privacy laws are stricter in the European Union and the ISO frameworks and certifications are more common there than in the United States. Suppose you took a position to work in Dublin or Hong Kong, for example. In that case, there may be experience and certification requirements that are specific to those regions that you would need to have before applying for those positions. So, yes, your career in cybersecurity is portable, but this is where my previous discussion about continuous education comes in. You will need to factor in education and certifications unique to where you would like to travel. I like to think this gives you more opportunities and adds to your portfolio of experience.

Just an Island Boy Finding Out About Technology ~ Chris

I was always passionate about information technology, since I was a young boy growing up in the Caribbean. While we did not have access to the latest and greatest technologies, by the year 2000, we had cable TV and the Internet. Some had 56k dial-up connections, which usually got more like 24-32k. A select few had blazing DSL at 128k. Since I was a teenager, I looked for something to do during my holidays and summers. Most of the time I ended up in an Internet cafe/computer store, not playing games or surfing the web, but helping to troubleshoot and repair clients' computers.

I quickly started to notice how poor security practices led to repeat customers, and usually for the same problems over and over again. Things like using the same passwords across many accounts, and not being careful about the type of information they posted online.

One of the many clients I had kept complaining that their friends and contacts were getting weird messages from them, and although they did not send them, they were still showing up in the Sent folder of their email mailbox. After some investigation, they informed me that it started happening a couple of days ago, and it was after they got a weird message on Myspace. When they went to log in to their Myspace account, it kept saying that their password was not working. But they were sure it was the right password. They eventually gave up and didn't think any more of it.

It turns out they were entering their username and password into a password stealer masquerading as the Myspace login page. To make matters worse, the same username/password combination they were using for Myspace was also what they used for their email service and several other sites. I strongly encouraged them to change all their passwords for the sites that used the same username/password combination and encouraged them to use long, memorable passwords for each service. I told them to write them down and save the document in a secured space, like a vault, to act as a backup for their memory. This was over 18 years ago, and password managers were not really a thing then. Today my advice would be slightly different.

Another example – I had a client that would get malware at least once a month. It turned out that this always stemmed from their use of music-sharing services. Apparently, they never scanned the files to see if they were infected or not. I advised them of the risk that viruses and malware posed to their machines and their data. I told them how to back up their systems and explained some of the things they could do to minimize the risk of getting their files infected. I also provided recommendations on anti-virus/anti-malware solutions to scan their machines for infestations.

Unfortunately, they did not take my advice to heart. The got infected with malware a couple more times, and eventually, they got a virus that corrupted their operating system, and they lost all their data. That last infection, which totally destroyed their system, is when my advice finally sunk in. That was when I realized I wanted to be in information security, to help people with these kinds of recurring and sometimes devastating problems. But, living in the Caribbean, I did not know there was such a job and could not imagine myself in such a career.

In this chapter, I will highlight some of the core themes I have noticed in my career that might help those considering a career in cybersecurity.

1. Passion for the field will endure over hard work

One of my mentors along the way shared with me that I can work hard and be just ok, or I can work hard at something that I am passionate about and produce amazing results. This lesson was something I took to heart in 2007 when the financial crisis caused the U.S. economy to collapse. I was in a sales role for something that generated no passion for me. No matter how hard I worked, my results were just "ok."

That year, I quit my sales role and started my journey towards a future in cybersecurity. I decided that starting over in a time of critical uncertainty in a field I was passionate about would focus my drive and love for what I was doing and help push me through rough times. I started from the bottom doing troubleshooting, helpdesk, and technical support, but over time I began assisting businesses in making secure decisions in their digital transformations.

There are so many different areas within this field to either generalize or specialize in; you must find out which works best for you. Find out what makes you excited to wake up in the morning and want to start the day versus going through the motions to get to 5 pm or the weekend. Find out what makes you want to go above and beyond, help someone else, learn something new every day, and get excited about what you can master tomorrow. With all that there is to learn in this field, you also need to accept that something you mastered five years ago can become obsolete tomorrow. Your love for the process must drive you. The joy of seeing the impact of your actions must be one of your primary motivators. The material rewards alone cannot sustain you.

It was not an easy road for me. I faced a lot of rejection while looking for new roles in a challenging economy, not exactly known for a thriving technology or security job market. But I didn't let that slow me down. Over the years, I changed roles intending to learn new things, moved to new parts of the country to have new experiences, and found that I also loved helping people get into this industry. I used many of the ideas, concepts, and recommendations that I will share later in this book on my journey, and I wanted to help write this book to share that advice with you. I know that you, too, can be successful in getting started in cybersecurity.

The demand for talented cybersecurity professionals is so high that there will be close to 3 million unfilled jobs by 2021.[1] No matter the number, it is a hot market, and many positions in the U.S. pay above the U.S. median wage.[2] [3] If you think that this is a field that interests you, be sure that you are entering it for the right reasons. While it could be a very lucrative field once you have started to hone your skills, it can also be a very stressful field, leading to significant rates of burnout. So don't do it just for the money; if that is your sole source of motivation it might not be worth it for you in the long run.

2. You define your own path

There are many roads into this industry, and while it might be easiest to take a defined path, it is still not that simple with cybersecurity. Some of the roles within the cybersecurity field are still in their infancy. While there might be a general understanding of some of the common roles, there are still many differences in opinion as to what is required to accomplish those roles. And, because there is so much demand for cybersecurity professionals, companies have created hybrid roles that require skills and competencies from many different roles such as IT, Software Development, and Audit/Governance.

This mismatch can be both a blessing and a curse for potential candidates. On the one hand, you can demonstrate to employers how you use different skills from various specialties or interests to solve a wide range of problems. However, if employers are focused on getting a specific set of skills, it begins to narrow your opportunities quickly. To overcome that obstacle, candidates often try to learn as much as they can about various technologies and end up not

---

[1] https://www.csoonline.com/article/3200024/cybersecurity-labor-crunch-to-hit-35-million-unfilled-jobs-by-2021.html
[2] https://resources.infosecinstitute.com/how-much-can-i-make-in-cybersecurity/
[3] https://www.bls.gov/ooh/computer-and-information-technology/information-security-analysts.htm

mastering any. They might also try to master a handful of skills and then develop a peripheral knowledge of others. It is up to you to decide which path you want to take.

Do you want to specialize or generalize? That was the question I asked myself. On the one hand, I loved technology (not just one area, but learning about many different areas) and helping people. On the other hand, I realized that if I did not find a way to stand out from the crowd, I would be in danger of simply blending in. I didn't want to blend in. Ultimately, I chose to generalize because I wanted to ensure that I would have a solid understanding of the connection between people and processes with the technology involved.

You might be asking yourself, what does that really mean? For me, that means that I want to understand why people are doing the things they do, and how their choices affect their decisions. For example, why does someone opt to use the season and year as their password? They could instead use something complex, like they were taught. It usually boils down to realizing that they were taught not to write down their passwords and that their passwords needed to be over eight characters with caps, numbers, and symbols. Therefore, something like "Spring2020!" would meet those requirements. With a solid understanding of how people think, the processes involved, and the available technologies, we can find ways to alleviate some of those concerns. In this case, by including a password manager on their machine. The password manager would help them create complex passwords (one for each account), remember them, and remove the urge to reuse the same password across many digital properties.

In very simple terms, this is how I approach problems. First, I seek to understand the situation (that people have a hard time creating complex passwords) and the complication (that people on average have more than 200 digital properties which they need to create a unique password for). Then I create a resolution that is as frictionless as possible for their work processes (allowing a password manager to help them create and remember unique complex passwords for their digital properties).

For me, that means that I need to know a little information about numerous disciplines, which means that I would have a hard time standing out in a crowd because I am a generalist. So, I chose to focus that generalization on helping people and companies with their digital transformations. In this case, moving from analog or traditional IT approaches to using the flexibility and benefits of the cloud. Moving to the cloud is a lot harder than it sounds at first. You must understand the logic behind what they are doing, including any challenges they might have. Only then you can work on recommendations to optimize their processes without introducing too much risk into the processes. In migrating to the cloud, you also need to understand the shared responsibility in that model. Add to that, all the new capabilities and the configuration settings that are now the customer's responsibility to secure.

To sum up my approach, look around at the different roles or career tracks within cybersecurity and see which ones align with your passions and values, and give you that feeling of "this is the best job in the world, look at what I get to do." This approach is how I found my path; you can define your own.

3. Be continuously curious

Many security professionals could be considered a "Renaissance person" because they need to have a little knowledge about how many things work, such as how to combine technology, people, and processes to produce a secure environment. You must be curious about all that is involved with the systems you are trying to secure, what goals the business is trying to achieve, and what is needed to help make the people involved aware of the risks and make the appropriate decisions. I am of the generalist mindset when it comes to security. I like to know a little or a lot about all the elements of the system. This curiosity means continuously learning about new technologies, process changes, and ways to influence people to achieve the desired outcome.

As mentioned in the previous section, while I generally focus on the people and process, with a solid understanding of the technology, I try to specialize in securing people and companies as they look to use cloud services to help make themselves and their business function more efficiently. From the perspective of being continuously curious, cybersecurity is an excellent field for you. Think about all the recent advances in cloud technologies.

There is so much to learn, from the best way to secure your digital assets to the best ways to manage your digital identities. And if that is not enough for you, each of the different cloud providers might do things in a slightly different way. While the principles don't change, you will need to consider the nuances of a particular cloud service in the recommendations you present to your clients. All these different nuances in technology and the continuous changes in the field make cybersecurity an excellent career for those who are curious.

The field of security has grown so large that it is no longer practical or even feasible for someone to master all the different specialties. There are so many different domains within the field that you are likely to find one or two areas that you are passionate about and several where you will be able to engage your curiosity and build new skills for years to come.

If you are curious, continuously learning, love challenges, and are a tinkerer by nature, you will find this field extremely interesting, and hopefully, you will learn to enjoy it too! However, if your primary drive is to get one of those high salaries in the industry and get rich quick, I am sorry to inform you that it takes a long time to get to that level, and if you don't have the passion and drive that I described, you will likely have a hard time and burn out.

Have fun, live, and learn.

Anyone Can Have a Career in Cybersecurity ~ Renee

In the summer of 2017, a high school invited me to speak to the students at a cyber summer camp about careers in cybersecurity. The career counselor and coordinator told me that the students tend to want to know what salary they can make if, and when, they start their cyber careers. They prepped me about the students wanting to learn about a day in the life of a "cyber pro," and many of them were looking for ways to shadow someone in cybersecurity as well as high school internships.

The career counselor shared with me that there were two groups of students combined for this talk. We were about to expose some kids to cyber concepts for the very first time. But some kids were in the advanced camp. These are kids who had some exposure already and may have taken that camp the year before. Many of them would be enrolled at the school, and others had come from other high schools or middle schools for this camp.

As I prepared for this talk, I thought back to when I was in high school and what I would be interested in hearing. I was like the current kids in that I would want to learn about what a day in the life of a security professional is like, how many years of education I would need, and how much money I would make. I decided to home in on my life as a human resources professional who turned into a cybersecurity professional and then blended the knowledge and experiences from both to launch a cyber recruitment company.

I walked into the jam-packed classroom, and the kids were buzzing with energy. Many were still working on their laptops and chatting until one of the teachers told them to settle down. I started by telling my story of how I have been a recruiter for many years in the technology space and then started recruiting in cybersecurity. I then shared that the cyber leaders who I had helped build their teams asked me to join the cybersecurity department, and I took on the challenge. Although I was very experienced in recruiting and some other areas of technology, I explained how I was now a newbie again, just like them, and had to learn new skills to do this new cyber job. I led a team of analysts in this new role, so I needed to learn what they did and then be able to answer their questions.

As I was reading the crowd, I saw many of them leaning in as I shared my story. The students had a lot of questions, including the ones the career counselor had shared. They wanted to know how quickly I learned these new skills, what it was like being in security monitoring, and did I need any certifications. They also asked about the pay. One student wanted to know the name of my book, and he quickly looked it up on Amazon, noted to me that it had 5-star reviews, nodded, and gave me a look of approval. I now had this 16-year old's approval, and it made me laugh.

More than anything, one comment moved me the most. There were a few young women in the room, and the career counselor asked if any of them had questions or comments. One young woman said that her parents had picked this camp for her, and she really wasn't interested when she began; however, she was learning a lot and starting to like it. She added that now, since I came and shared my story and path to security, she would consider it as a profession. It warmed my heart to hear her say that.

I tell this story to illustrate a few things:

- If those middle school and high school students were learning the basics of cybersecurity in a summer camp, you can too. As much as many people try to make it seem like learning a foreign language or becoming a rocket scientist, some areas of cybersecurity are not that difficult to learn.
- A career in cybersecurity may seem like it's only about being super "techie" like coding or engineering, but that's not the case.

- You may not know if a career in cybersecurity is for you until you hear a story of someone's career that resonates with you like mine resonated for that young woman.
- Determining if a career in cybersecurity is for you is more about assessing your skills and passions and aligning them to the myriad of disciplines within the cybersecurity career field.

I believe everyone can have a career in cybersecurity.

Learning about cybersecurity like a middle schooler

When I initially started recruiting cybersecurity professionals, I had no idea what the profession was about. I first had to learn the nuances of what it meant to be in the cybersecurity department and what the various areas of cybersecurity did daily. At the time, I sat with multiple leaders and had them explain what each role did. I literally said to them, "Explain this to me like I was five years old." Those leaders quickly went from teaching me what I considered a foreign language to explaining in very practical terms what each department and role did. They were able to share analogies that I immediately understood, and that helped me gain clarity for the roles I needed to recruit for them.

At this point, everyone should have a basic understanding of cybersecurity for personal safety. Especially since the 2020 pandemic, with millions of people forced to work from home, there is a higher sense of urgency to do so. You can learn much of the basics the same way we teach middle and high schoolers. An entry into cybersecurity in this manner can provide you with a higher-level overview of what it is and the various components that make it up.

Learning about cybersecurity through programs like HackerHighSchool.org or Cybrary can provide the basics in an easily digestible format. A quick YouTube or Google search will provide you with high-level overviews of Cybersecurity 101, and other books in this series do the same.

Acquiring a knowledge of the basics is the first step to understanding what cybersecurity is and determining what interests you the most and where you could potentially fit in.

A career in cybersecurity is not only for coders and super "techie" people

This fear is probably one of the biggest myths when it comes to cybersecurity. You do not need to know how to code to be in cybersecurity, although knowing how to code will help tremendously in your career.

I co-host a podcast called *Breaking into Cybersecurity*, and we have interviewed over 100 guests who have recently transitioned into their first job in cybersecurity. The diversity of their skills and professional backgrounds before their first cybersecurity job shows the seemingly limitless number of skills helpful in breaking into the industry. We have had a librarian, a hospital operating room technician, an Uber driver, a waitress, and a high school student all successfully break into cybersecurity, and I don't believe any of them consider themselves coding experts or "techies."

According to a recent EC-Council blog, there are many technical and non-technical skills needed to succeed in cybersecurity. Some of the non-tech skills include communication skills, analytical thinking skills, determination, and most importantly, a passion for continuous learning. I barely made it out of a C programming class almost two decades ago, and I was able to become a successful security lead, so don't let a lack of technical skills deter you from a career in cybersecurity. You can pick up those skills along the way.

Learn about various career pathways to security

Like the high school student mentioned above, you may not have initially considered a career in cybersecurity, but something made you curious. And while there are likely hundreds or even thousands like you, this book is for you, and we're here to help you on your journey.

Don't let the lack of "cybersecurity career awareness" in general and the even more significant lack of awareness of how people with a variety of skills and backgrounds have successfully entered a career in cybersecurity deter you. A few ways to learn about how people with different skill sets or from a multitude of backgrounds have gotten their start in cybersecurity: check out the *Breaking into Cybersecurity* podcast and Cybercrime Magazine's podcast, and read *Cybersecurity Career Guide: Who Works in Cybersecurity, How We Got Started, Why We Need You.*

Additional resources that show pathways to an entry-level role and career progression in security include cyberseek.org and CompTIA's Career Pathways. Both resources show the skills needed and recommended certifications for entry and progression in the field.

What Color is Your Parachute?

The book, *What Color is Your Parachute?* known as the "Career Bible" in HR circles and university career services centers, has sold more than 10 million copies over 50 years. As summarized in its book description:

> "When *What Color Is Your Parachute?* was first published in 1970, it revolutionized the concept of job hunting. Unlike traditional guides to the job market, it helped job seekers understand themselves first, then find the jobs that fit, using a mix of good-humored advice and practical strategy."[4]

The emphasis here is on helping job seekers understand themselves first. Understanding your strengths and what comes naturally to you will make your path to a career in cybersecurity, or any career, so

---
[4] Katharine Brooks, EdD, Introduction to 2021 Edition

much easier. Taking inventory of what you spend time doing when you have free time is one of the keys to determining what you may want to do in your career. Additional resources for career assessments are the book StengthsFinder 2.0 by Tom Rath and the Department of Labor's O*Net Career Exploration Tools. These resources will help you narrow down the types of careers that will be the best fit for you. You can then target those to careers in cybersecurity to see where you would best fit.

In closing, cyber can be a career for anyone. The question is determining your strengths and passions coupled with how they align to the various components of cyber. This is an excellent way to see where you would fit in.

Resources:

- https://blog.eccouncil.org/skills-that-you-require-to-pursue-a-career-in-cybersecurity/
- https://cybersecurityventures.com/
- https://www.paloaltonetworks.com/resources/ebooks/cybersecurity-career-guide
- https://www.comptia.org/certifications/which-certification
- https://www.parachutebook.com/
- https://www.gallup.com/cliftonstrengths/en/strengthsfinder.aspx

Chapter 1 – Key Points and Recommended Actions

The following is a quick summary of the key points from this chapter:

- Cybersecurity is a vast domain that encompasses many disciplines. This leads to a lot of opportunities and a great many skills that one can leverage to break into the field.
- The field of cybersecurity is ever evolving and requires a mindset of continuous learning.
- Cybersecurity is not just for highly technical engineers. Almost any job discipline is transferrable to cybersecurity at some level.
- The first place to start learning is to learn how to secure yourself – your personal equipment and your access to apps – this generates a fundamental cyber-awareness that can be the beginning of your journey.
- Volunteer while you are doing your formal learning. You can gain valuable technical experience as you learn the skills you'll need to succeed.
- Cybersecurity is more mission-focused than most fields. While it typically pays above average, the dedication required and the inherent stress of always playing defense means money alone is rarely enough. Shared mission is essential.

Here is a recommended first step you can take to start the process of developing your cybersecurity knowledge:

- Physician, heal thyself.[5] Take an inventory of your devices, apps, online accounts, and all the technology you consume.

---

[5] Dating back to ancient Greece, the chorus says to Prometheus in Prometheus Bound: "Like an unskilled doctor, fallen ill, you lose heart and cannot discover by which remedies to cure your own disease." The moral of the proverb is to attend to one's own defects before those in others.

Research how to secure each device and proceed to secure your digital life. For extra credit, help your friends and family secure their digital lives as well.

Section 2

Self-Assessment

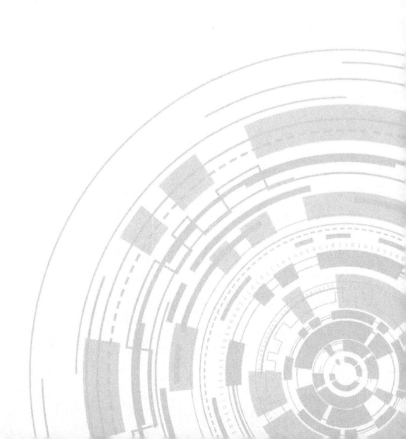

Introduction

"At the center of your being, you have the answer; you know who you are, and you know what you want."

This quote is attributed to Lao Tzu, possibly a Chinese philosopher who, if he existed, is credited with founding Taoism around 500 BCE. It was a long time ago. We're not sure. But we are sure that you must know who you are before creating a plan to develop your career in cybersecurity.

In the following three chapters, we're going to go on a journey of self-discovery. There is no need to panic. This journey is not a new-wave exercise of navel-gazing. Instead, we're going to provide some practical advice for doing an honest assessment of how you stack up as a candidate for cybersecurity jobs.

It starts with what is important to you. Gary, Chris, and Renee share their passions for cybersecurity. The sense of community that is present within our ranks is frankly refreshing in the modern world. Next comes an assessment of skills and capabilities. You'll want an honest inventory of the skills you have that translate to a job in this field. Along with this, we'll provide recommendations for practical ways to close the gaps you'll uncover. Finally, we'll provide our opinions on the must-have soft skills you'll need to be successful. Cybersecurity is a team sport, and teams must share certain traits to be successful.

"Knowing yourself is the beginning of all wisdom," said Aristotle. By the time you've finished this section, we're sure you'll be a little wiser.

Chapter 2

Where to Begin?

Introduction

From the previous chapter, you should now have some insight into the field of cybersecurity and how it is comprised of numerous domains consisting of different technologies, industries, and job types. As you finished that chapter, we hope you were excited to realize that cybersecurity is a fascinating career field with an opportunity just waiting for you to get started. Then reality knocked on your door as you realized how vast this new world looks to you, and the question driving the title for this chapter hit you – where do I begin?

Understand that just about everyone who works in cybersecurity has had that feeling of panic and asked themselves the same question. We designed this chapter to help you start answering that question. We describe our own experiences and methodologies to begin planning our careers and selecting a particular work domain.

As we begin, we want to say that everyone's experiences and the methods they use to develop their career plan are different. Honestly, that diversity is what makes the cybersecurity career field and community so attractive. So please dive in, take some notes, and begin to envision where you want to start in cybersecurity. Don't forget that we are a community, so if you have questions or feel you are stuck, that's ok; just reach out and ask for help. We have all been where you are right now. That first step looks daunting, but once you start walking down your path, you won't even remember how worried you were. Let's get started.

My Path to a Career in Cybersecurity ~ Gary

When I started my US Navy career many years ago, I was assigned a job in the advanced electronics field. I had originally tested and asked for computers, but you don't always get what you want as many veterans can attest. With that said, I was happy with my assigned choice. I did get the chance to work with computers, and I honestly thought my career would be as an electrical engineer. However, several years later, by chance, I read a book that would impact me professionally and motivate me to change my mind and focus on a new career.

The book *Information Warfare* was written by Winn Schwartau. After reading it, I became fascinated with not just computers but the idea of how global networks of computers could be used for dual purposes. That book started me down a long, twisted path full of questions, and years later, I find I am still walking that path and I am truly enjoying the experience. Our discussion for this chapter will focus on my progress, and how I made changes to pivot into a career in cybersecurity. Hopefully, this information will be helpful as you establish your career in cybersecurity.

Information Technology (IT) today permeates every facet of our daily lives. We would be very hard-pressed to find a place in the world where local citizens or their governments use no technology. I believe we must judge this growth of technology by the negative and positive impacts on society. Technology is just a tool, but a tool with seemingly infinite uses for both good and evil. It is this dual aspect of technology that brought me into the field of cybersecurity. I found the more I developed my career in IT, the more I sought to expand my experience and knowledge in security. Then one day, I just decided to step over and fully accept security as my chosen career.

I am like many people in cybersecurity who, from a young age, were continuously playing with computers and learning through experience about this amazing new digital world. However, my career really began with a lab I built in my garage. I made way too many shopping trips to computer stores and online sites for spare parts. When the dust settled in my garage, I had a full rack of network routers and switches plus several rows of networked Windows and Linux desktops and servers (pre-virtualization days – I feel old because most of this can now be done virtually). I would use this equipment over many long nights to teach myself networking, a little hacking (who am I kidding? a lot of hacking), network operations, and computer forensics. I also used this lab to help me study for my first certifications, and as my career progressed, I would reconfigure the lab to study for new certifications that matched my new job roles.

This lab provided me with a platform to teach myself new skills. One skill that I still use today is the idea of mind-mapping an end goal and then developing a staged approach to achieving it. To begin this process, you would typically note what skills you currently have and which ones you lack to achieve your goal. With that knowledge, you then begin building a career plan. I have found it helpful to develop a project roadmap that you break into smaller, integrated segments. Each segment is like a mini project designed to help you achieve a skill set, certification, or experience in an area you believe you will need to complete your greater goal. I want to point out that once you develop this career map, don't get discouraged by how long it may take you to complete it. Accept that it will take time to achieve your long-term goals. Focus on your first step, put your head down, and get to work.

Now back to my story. As I mentioned, I used this lab to experiment and increase my knowledge of IT and cybersecurity. I used it to learn how things work, sometimes breaking things, and then researching methods to correct my errors. Sometimes, humbling though it was, I learned I was not as smart as I thought, and I would have to ask for help. What's important to note here is that I spent time, over several years, working in this lab and taking any classes I could find at my local universities or junior colleges. I developed my career mind-map, a process I still use to this day. This mind-map consisted of a certification tree where I mapped out what certifications, skills, and experience I would need to acquire if I wanted to apply for a specific role such as Network Engineer or Security Architect. The reason for developing this mind-map was that I wanted to document a methodical process that I could follow over time to ensure that I would meet the requirements for a job in cybersecurity. I developed my career map by beginning with several tools, including a security certifications mind-map, and references such as employment and networking websites, and education and career websites.

This chapter is centered on how I used my IT and security certifications mind-map and employment and networking websites to develop a list of required skills and experience for future positions. Before I get started, I want to say I am by no means an expert. This chapter is based on what I have learned over the last 20 years as my career progressed in both IT and cybersecurity. I believe my experience in having moved through multiple disciplines within the IT and cybersecurity fields gives me a unique perspective on the experience and insight a senior security professional gains from having a broad range of IT knowledge. With that said, I will describe some of the tools and web sites I used to help me in my career and why I used them. It is my hope this knowledge will help you as well. Let's get started.

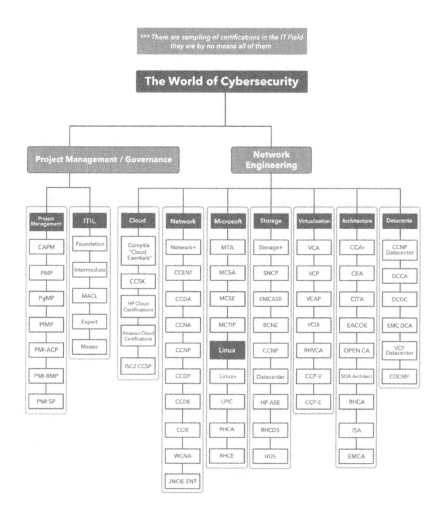

Figure 2.1 Cybersecurity Certification Mind-Map (part 1)

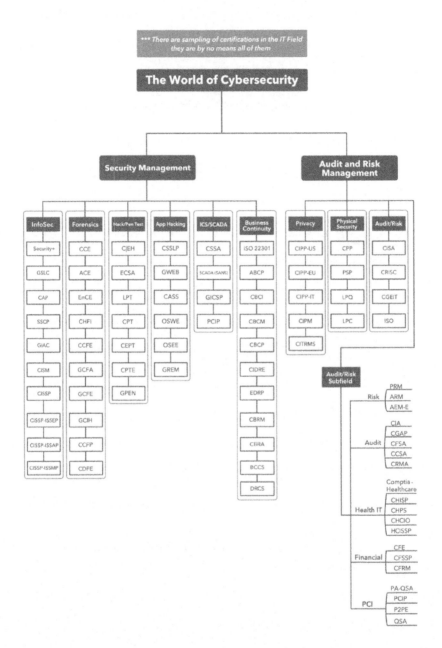

Figure 2.2 Cybersecurity Certification Mind-Map (Part 2)

I created the two-part diagram as a mind map which I called "The World of Cybersecurity."[6] In this document I researched the certifications and domains that were grouped within the greater career field of cybersecurity. The certifications I listed in these domain areas are by no means all that are available, they are only examples that I documented so I could understand that if I focused on a career in a specific domain such as Security Engineering there would be several technologies and certifications I would need to learn to be an effective security engineer. This diagram is available for download if you are creating your own career map. Even though it is several years old it's a good template to get you started.

The main idea I want to convey with this diagram is that I tried to break the cybersecurity career field into five main fields of study. They are:

- Network Management/Security Operations
- Network/Security Engineering
- Information Security
- Audit/Risk Management
- Application Security

Please note that under each of these "fields of study" are sub-groups and inside these are numerous disciplines that one can delve into and find an area of interest. What's important to note here is that there are plenty of disciplines to choose from. I know numerous people who, like myself, are multi-disciplined and have worked at times across several of the fields I have listed in this diagram. A good reference you can use to update this template to reflect what you are interested in would be the NICE Cybersecurity Workforce Framework.[7]

---

[6] https://app.box.com/Path-to-Cyber-slides
[7] https://niccs.cisa.gov/workforce-development/cyber-security-workforce-framework

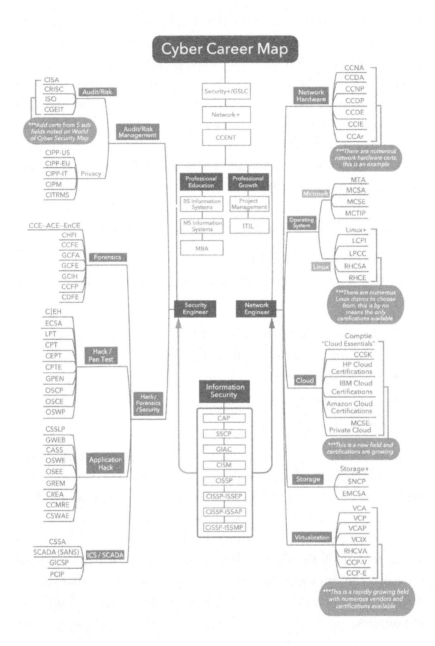

Figure 2.3 Cybersecurity Career Map

After I had finished creating the cybersecurity certification mindmap, I then built a career map where I tried to factor in certification, education, and experience that I believed I would need as my career progressed. I would, later in my career, use similar versions of this document when mentoring my teams and peers to help them efficiently document their current progress and highlight the next steps they might wish to take in their careers.

Note how I put networking on one side of this diagram and security on the other. I created my career map this way because I knew I would need networking experience, so I factored in having to work in IT and progressing to security. I found out much of this from reviewing security job requirements on employment sites and speaking with security professionals already in the field. Through discussions with peers, I have found that many of us started in IT or some IT-related field and worked our way into security. With my career map, I planned for that. As you can see in this second diagram, it starts at the top as an entry-level employee where I list several basic certifications that I believe provide foundational knowledge for those new to IT or Cybersecurity. After the basic certifications, I segmented my career map into five areas:

- Security Engineer
- Network Engineer
- Information Security
- Professional Education
- Professional Growth

How I envision you might use this diagram is after you complete your basic certifications, you would select an arm of the diagram, left for "Security Engineer" or right for "Network Engineer." Over time, as you gain some experience and continue to work on the certifications listed under the section you selected, you would also choose a certification from "Information Security."

I originally put this certification tree together to use as a visual map, enabling me to see the flow of certifications, experience, and skillsets in specific areas that I found interesting. It also would help me see the succession of requirements I would need to complete as I moved up in my career. I use this map when I peruse employment sites. When I see, for instance, that a specific job description states a requirement to hold a CCNP certification, I know from looking at my map there are prerequisite certifications and experience that I would need to complete first. I would know, therefore, that I don't yet qualify for that job. Before we move on, I want to note that this diagram is also downloadable and if you use it to create your own career map, remember that it's not set in stone. These career maps are flexible and are designed to let you document new requirements, technologies, and required skills. Using this tool, you will have a continuously updated reminder of what you need to achieve your goal. The critical point here is that this process is continuous.

Where to Begin?

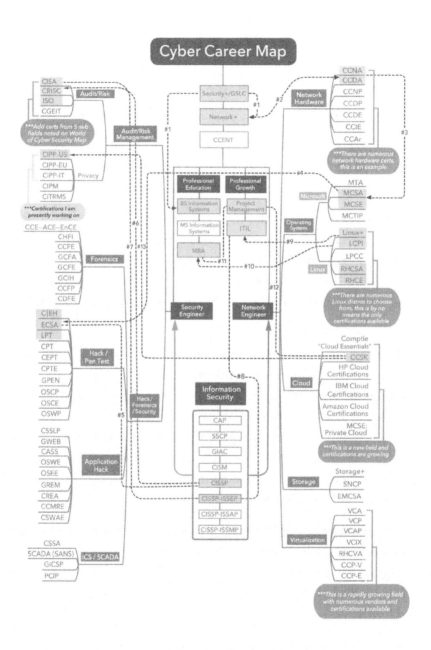

Figure 2.4 Cybersecurity Career Map (Actual)

Our final diagram, shown above, is an actual career map. This map represents my career, detailed out as an example. As you can see from this diagram, the certifications and degrees highlighted in light gray are the ones I have completed over the last 20 years of my career. I put the "Professional Education" piece in the center of the diagram because over my career, I completed my education in parallel with certifications that I was working on. You can see in the diagram that I started with two of the three basic certs (Security+, Network+, CCENT) and then moved into the Network Engineer track first.

As a network engineer, I did my Cisco certifications then proceeded to learn operating systems. I found doing the Cisco certifications first actually helped me because I understood how networks are put together and how data flowed in enterprise networks, and I had a good understanding of protocols before I got into specific operating systems.

As I gained more experience and started to manage teams, I became very interested in doing network penetration testing, so I started working on certifications in the Hacking & Pentesting group. After completing several of those certifications, I had close to ten years of experience working on enterprise IT networks and knew I had enough experience to qualify for the CISSP certification. So, I decided to work on it and marked it off as noted in the above career map in the Information Security group.

The main point to note looking at this diagram is that I worked on both sides in multiple areas. Many of these changes were directed by changes in my employment. However, I selected certifications in the various fields of experience because of research into specific job descriptions.

I did much of this research about specific jobs by joining professional organizations such as ISSA or ISACA to better understand the various fields in IT and Cybersecurity. While talking with members, I would sometimes hear about a job that sounded interesting, and I could envision myself being a good fit for it. I would access job boards and career websites and look for job descriptions that matched this interesting job. Reading the descriptions of the roles, I would note the experience required and any required certifications. I would use this information as a blueprint to update my "Cybersecurity Career Map" and then assess where I was currently on this map and what I still needed to complete if I wanted to apply for that particular type of job. As I educated myself on the cybersecurity career field, I also found that particular soft skills seemed mandatory in every job description I reviewed. I took this knowledge and added it to my career map. I mention this because it's essential for you to understand the career equation: **soft skills + tech skills + experience = Job.** Don't miss one of those components when creating your career map.

In conclusion, please keep in mind that the information I have provided is to help you begin your journey. Starting on this path will take time. You will not be a cybersecurity professional overnight. Many of you may also have some previous IT/Cybersecurity experience and education and are just looking to fine-tune your progress as you prepare to transition your career to the next level. Either way, as you progress, please continue your education. I would also recommend you continue to seek hands-on experience in building some computers or networks (hardware or virtual), play with some operating systems and cloud, and volunteer at some non-profits or security community events. The big thing to remember is don't quit. Make sure you go to some of the chapter meetings of your local IT and cybersecurity professional organizations and network with people there and ask for their advice. Ask them whom would they recommend you go to for experience? How did they get their experience and training? Do they know any exciting jobs you should look at? Can they review your résumé and make recommendations for improvement? Keep asking these questions. Use any answers that you find suitable for you to adjust your cybersecurity career map and keep moving forward.

Finding Your Passion ~ Chris

As you take this journey to find your passion, you will want to do some **self-discovery.** You may want to ask yourself some questions like:

- What about the cybersecurity field interests you? What types of roles?
- What is so interesting about that role?
- Is there someone accomplished in the field that you look up to? Why? What about them and their role makes you look up to them?

Many do not realize how truly vast the cybersecurity field is, which causes them to overlook many aspects of the field which do not align with the stereotypical view of a cybersecurity career. Below is a depiction of the primary cybersecurity domains.

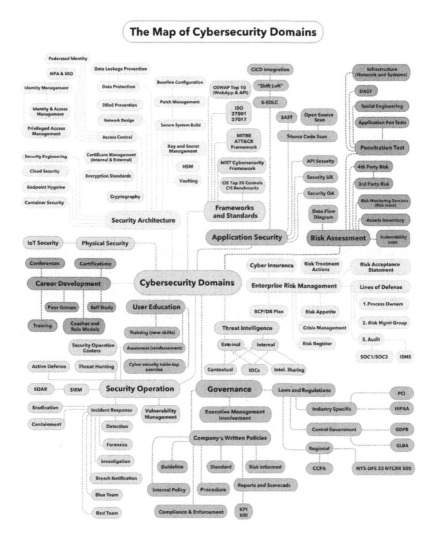

Figure 2.5 Derived from Map of Cybersecurity Domains V3.0 - Courtesy Henry Jiang

I provide this domain map because when you get to the root of why you are interested in this field, you can then target your path into this industry.

1. Types of Roles

Cybersecurity as a field has a broad range of job types, including awareness and training, testing for vulnerabilities, assessing risk within an environment, developing policies and procedures, auditing those items, and many more. Those considering a career within this field should think about what piece of the wheel they are passionate about and focus on becoming great at it. Once you have mastered your area of focus, or perhaps when you realize that it would not be the best use of your time, you can always choose another area to focus on. By then, you'll have your foot in the door.[8]

If you are unsure which area you'd like to focus on, you can start by researching a particular role or sector, reading job descriptions, and seeing if those items interest you. Below is an example of some of the titles you can find in cybersecurity from security ventures.[9]

---

[8] Thanks to the National Initiative for Cybersecurity Careers and Studies (NICCS) from whom this section draws heavily.
[9] https://cybersecurityventures.com/50-cybersecurity-titles-that-every-job-seeker-should-know-about/

Cybersecurity Job Titles

1. Application Security Administrator - Keep software / apps safe and secure.
2. Artificial Intelligence Security Specialist - Use AI to combat cybercrime.
3. Automotive Security Engineer - Protect cars from cyber intrusions.
4. Blockchain Developer / Engineer - Code the future of secure transactions.
5. Blue Team Member - Design defensive measures / harden operating systems.
6. Bug Bounty Hunter - Freelance hackers find defects and exploits in code.
7. Cybersecurity Scrum Master - Watch over and protect all data.
8. Chief Information Security Officer (CISO) - Head honcho of cybersecurity.
9. Chief Security Officer (CSO) - Head up all physical/info/cyber security.
10. Cloud Security Architect - Secure apps and data in the cloud.
11. Counterespionage analyst - Thwart cyber spies from hostile nation states.
12. Cryptanalyst - Decipher coded messages without a cryptographic key.
13. Cryptographer - Develop systems to encrypt sensitive information.
14. Cyber Insurance Policy Specialist - Consult on cyber risk and liability protection.
15. Cyber Intelligence Specialist - Analyze cyber threats and defend against them.
16. Cyber Operations Specialist - Conduct offensive cyberspace operations.
17. Cybercrime Investigator - Solve crimes conducted in cyberspace.
18. Cybersecurity Hardware Engineer - Develop security for computer hardware.
19. Cybersecurity Lawyer - Attorney focused on info/cybersecurity and cybercrime.
20. Cybersecurity Software Developer / Engineer - Bake security into applications. ...

...

38. Network Security Administrator - Secure networks from internal and external threats.
39. Penetration Tester (Pen-Tester) - Perform authorized and simulated cyberattacks.
40. PKI (Public Key Infrastructure) Analyst - Manage secure transfer of digital information.
41. Red Team Member - Participate in real-world cyberattack simulations.
42. SCADA (Supervisory control and data acquisition)
    Security Analyst - Secure critical infrastructures.
43. Security Auditor - Conduct audits on an organization's information systems.
44. Security Awareness Training Specialist - Train employees on cyber threats.
45. Security Operations Center (SOC) Analyst - Coordinate and report on cyber incidents.
46. Security Operations Center (SOC) Manager - Oversee all SOC personnel.
47. Source Code Auditor - Analyze software code to find bugs, defects, and breaches.
48. Threat Hunter - Search networks to detect and isolate advanced threats.
49. Virus Technician - Detect and remediate computer viruses and malware.
50. Vulnerability Assessor - Find exploits in systems and applications.

Figure 2.6 Courtesy Cybersecurity Ventures

You will notice that this list focuses primarily on the more technical roles within the industry. Don't forget about the other roles supporting or assisting these functions, including sales, marketing, risk management, legal, and project management. Do not limit yourself to just these listed roles. The industry is evolving and still can surprise us. Don't be afraid to see a gap in what companies are trying to accomplish and suggest creating a bridge role between those two areas.

You can learn more about some of the roles that you are particularly interested in by having an informational interview with someone currently in that role or responsible for managing those who are. I will be providing more information on this topic later.

No matter where you are in your journey, there are different pathways into the industry or to grow within the industry. Below I will discuss a tool from National Initiative for Cybersecurity Careers and Studies (NICSS) that shows how different cyber roles relate to each other and how to use them to pivot from where you are in your career to where you might want to go.

From the NICSS website, NICSS's mission is to "be a hub that provides the tools and resources needed to ensure that the United States workforce has the appropriate training and education. It is managed by the Cybersecurity Defense Education and Training (CDET) subdivision within the Cybersecurity and Infrastructure Security Agency's (CISA) Cybersecurity Division which is part of the Department of Homeland Security (DHS). CDET promotes cybersecurity awareness, training, education, and career structure, with the added goal of broadening the Nation's volume of cybersecurity workforce professionals."[10]

The first resource under the NICSS you should consider is the NICE Framework,[11] which breaks down the different aspects of the cybersecurity profession into more manageable components,

---

[10] https://niccs.cisa.gov/about-niccs/learn-about-niccs
[11] https://niccs.us-cert.gov/workforce-development/cyber-security-workforce-framework

including categories, specialties, and roles. The NICE Framework is comprised of the following components:

- **Categories** – A high-level grouping of seven common cybersecurity functions
- **Specialty Areas** – 33 distinct areas of cybersecurity work
- **Work Roles** – The most detailed groupings (52 in all) of cybersecurity work consisting of the specific knowledge, skills, and abilities (KSAs) required to perform tasks in a work role.

Besides NICSS and the Nice Framework, DHS also led an effort to create a set of **Work Role Capability Indicators.** This set is a combination of education, certification, training, experiential learning, and continuous learning attributes that could indicate a greater likelihood of success for a given work role.

You can explore the different domains to find roles that align with your skills and experiences or find a dream role and work backward to learn the skills, training, and experiences you'll need to succeed in those roles.

1. How to Pivot from Your Existing Role

Let's discuss the different segments of the cyber workforce and how you can combine the skill sets you already have with the new skills you'll acquire to transition into a new role.[12]

The NICCS site provides several excellent resources, one of which, the Cyber Career Pathways tool, allows you to easily discover adjacencies to a role you might currently have or that you intend to use as your starting point for your cybersecurity career. As you explore these adjacencies, you'll be able to see how to fill the gaps

---

[12] https://niccs.us-cert.gov/workforce-development/cyber-career-pathways

between your current skill set and the skill set you'll need to move into the adjacent role.

Before you start to jump from where you are to where you think you want to go, I recommend that you find out whether it will be a good fit for you. I learned throughout my career that while a role might seem to apply from the outside looking in, it might not be as appealing once you get started. The discovery process is a crucial step to avoiding this trap.

2. Discovery Process: What about that role makes it so attractive?

In the previous section, we discussed some of the types of roles within the cybersecurity field, and that should provide you with an excellent foundation for self-discovery. Additionally, the last section also showed the interconnected nature of some of the roles. These tools can help you explore the possible paths to explore towards getting to a dream job or helping your transition from one area of cyber to another. For those who are not within cybersecurity, you can use them as a stepping-stone for reaching a dream role by looking at the positions that might be connected and more easily attained.

The critical aspect of this section is exploring the skills and competencies required for a specific position. For some roles, the clarity of what the role requires is still being defined. At the same time, other roles might be well developed. Unlike other fields, the cybersecurity field is still relatively new at 20-30 years old.

Many companies are still blending the skills and competencies from several different roles into one and giving a new position a similar-sounding job title. Therefore, it is essential to read the various job descriptions to see what they are asking for within the roles. I will also warn you that due to the immature nature of the industry, many companies have unrealistic expectations when it comes to requirements posted in job descriptions. Do not let that dissuade you from a role. Look at these job descriptions as a wish list of the skills and competencies critical to them. In the end, most companies will select a candidate who has the best mix of the requested qualifications at the time of hire.

For additional details consider reading:

NIST Special Publication 800-181 National Initiative for Cybersecurity Education (NICE) Cybersecurity Workforce Framework.[13]

3. Informational Interviews: What is it about the person you admire and their role that makes you look up to them?

Growing up in the Caribbean and then traveling around the world has been a fantastic experience for me. One of the most important lessons from my travels was to learn as much from the locals as possible. I discovered how to use their experiences and knowledge to make the most of my opportunities. This lesson applies to many aspects of life, and I am going to share how you can use these lessons in your journey into cybersecurity. At first, you might not know much about the roles, responsibilities, and challenges of a position. Uncovering this information is where you can use the technique of asking the locals or those currently in the roles for their insights. Try to gain as many insights as possible from them about their positions to see if it would be something in which you might be interested. You also want to ensure that you get a balanced approach, so you want to have these conversations with several different people to help rule out any biases or bad experiences one person might have had that don't translate to the role in general.

As part of your self-discovery process, you might want to look for role models in the industry. These can be individuals working for

---

[13] https://nvlpubs.nist.gov/nistpubs/SpecialPublications/NIST.SP.800-181.pdf?trackDocs=NIST.SP.800-181.pdf

companies you admire, working in roles you are interested in, or who are just experienced in the field. During this phase, the aim is to reach out to individuals in those roles or companies. Find out if they are willing to have an informational interview with you to learn more about their role, their specialty, or their company.

These conversations allow you to hear firsthand from someone in a role about what they do daily, the skills they need for a position, and the pressures they may face. From this you can start to decide whether you think this role might be a good fit for you. These conversations are your opportunity to dive deeper into different aspects of the topic you wanted to discuss. Some of the issues you might consider:

- What is it like in this type of role? Is it what you expected? What would the old you want to know about the role before you got into it?
- What are the problems they might face in their role/specialty/company?
- What do they do to overcome these types of issues? (i.e., What makes them successful?)
- What are some of the things they do to stand out from the crowd? (i.e., How do they stay one step ahead of the rest?)

The informational interview is your chance to learn as much as you can. Be respectful of their time; if you are allowed 30 minutes of time, do not go over. Instead, stop with a 5-minute gap and say that you appreciate their time in the interview, and thank them for their time. If you would like to stand out from the crowd, sending a kind note a couple of days later thanking them for their time goes a long way. It also helps build a possible long-term relationship with this experienced individual. They could be your future boss one day or be helpful in a future recommendation.

Keep in mind, this is not an actual interview, so there is no job at the end of this. However, you can use this conversation as a springboard for ongoing conversations. You can find out if they can help you gather more potential leads by asking about any companies hiring for the position you are seeking.

What Should Be Your First Steps? ~ Renee

"That Infosec group is tough. Many recruiters have been thrown out of there," said my colleague. "Recruiters being thrown out is hilarious," I replied, laughing. That's what my colleague said as he began to transition the open cybersecurity jobs to me. I was the recruiter taking on the infamous InfoSec department in our company. This department was known for having constant turnover and for jobs taking nine months to fill. My leader also gave me a pep talk about working with this group and how difficult it would be.

I initially thought this recruiter and team lead were overreacting. They had no idea what difficult recruiting was. I worked in investment banks where we would be yelled at daily for not having "our act together" but said in more colorful language. I pulled all-nighters to bring in dozens of software architect candidates for a recruiting day to ensure we hired people quickly for an immediate project. Every day that this project wasn't staffed, the bank lost money. The pressure was always on.

So far, nothing at this company came remotely close to my prior experiences of challenging recruiting searches. There was an occasional difficult search as I looked to fill quant analyst positions, but overall, it was smooth sailing. That all changed when I became the recruiting partner for Infosec. Learning how to recruit security professionals became one of the biggest challenges of my career. That group was tough for a multitude of reasons – the company's reputation at the time wasn't that good, the job market in the Washington, D.C. metro area was, and still is, one of the most in-demand markets for cybersecurity, and the pay was average. This combination created a perfect storm of reasons why someone would **not** be interested in these opportunities.

One day, I had a weekly status meeting with one of the Infosec directors. We reviewed a job that was especially difficult to fill. It had been open for nine months. "You could have trained me up to do this job in nine months," I jokingly said to the director, who eventually became the CISO. Fast forward a year, and there I was being trained to be a Security Monitoring Lead. That's how I broke into cybersecurity.

I used to think my story was unique. Who else had zero security experience and limited tech experience and was able to break into the field? After hosting over 100 episodes of the podcast, *Breaking into Cybersecurity*, I know that the answer is many. In fact, since cybersecurity degrees and certifications are relatively new, most security professionals came from a background other than cybersecurity.

Now I will begin to give you a combination of steps that many people took to break into their first security role, including what some leaders saw in the people they selected to transition into their cybersecurity department.

Assessments

As shared in Chapter 1, assessments are an excellent way to understand what makes you tick. Although I haven't heard of many people who do this as a first step in seeking a career in cybersecurity, I believe it should be. Knowing your strengths and weaknesses is essential for selecting the best role and setting yourself up for success. Understanding your personality and what drives you will help you narrow down the best security area for you. People at all levels should take assessments every few years to see if they have changed. Assessments are also helpful to understand your blind spots. You'll want to see yourself with all your flaws to determine what you should do next in your career and what jobs are the best fit for you.

The military's ASVAB test is the one that all new military recruits must take. The Department of Defense is also piloting a new entrance exam called the TAPAS test to assess any potential increase in the quality of recruits. These tests are specifically for entrants into the armed forces, so the general public cannot take them; however, there are many assessments on the market that private sector employers, universities, and individuals have used.

CareerOneStop is your best source for career exploration, training, and jobs. The U.S. Department of Labor sponsors the site. They have an "Explore Careers" tab on their website that takes you straight to self-assessments. They also explain what's in an assessment and the various assessments that they provide. Their "Interest Assessment" is a quick way to narrow down careers that may be a fit. The assessment will provide a wide array of professions and their outlook, hourly wage, and the education needed. As noted on their site, the Interest Assessment is based on O* NET's profiler.

O*NET is also sponsored by the Department of Labor and provides a more in-depth analysis of the job market and assessments. Along with their assessment tool at mynextmove.org, they have a "Hot Technologies" section and a "Veterans" section dedicated to helping veterans transfer their military skills to the private and government sectors. There is a wealth of information on this site, including a section called "Careers with a Bright Outlook" that provides a list of rapidly growing careers that are in demand.

According to their book description, in 2007, The Economist listed the book StrengthsFinder 2.0 as the top-selling business book worldwide. This book helps people uncover their talents and includes access to their online assessment, now known as the CliftonStrengths Assessment. This book, along with its online assessments, is one of my favorites as it provides a quick overview of your strengths and explains how the people with the most successful careers focus on careers where their strengths dominate.

Although these are only a sampling of my favorites, feel free to explore the list of assessments provided in the resources section and others you may like. The goal is to take an assessment and learn about the job that best fits you.

Industry Assessments

Just as we advise you to take a self-assessment, we recommend assessing the industry since there are numerous pathways for entering the cybersecurity field based on where you are in your career. The cybersecurity industry is vast, and there is a place for everyone. One of the ways to transition into cybersecurity is to become laser-focused on where you'd like to be and where your current skills best match and reverse engineer the process to get into that position.

There are three common ways to transition to security. The first is considered early career entry. Early career entry is the path from high school or college and is most often a person's first or second job in their career. The second and third ways are mid-career transitions. We define mid-career transitions as either transitioning from another industry while keeping your current career or transitioning from another job within the same company. In this section, we will delve into all three.

Entry-level

If you are lucky enough to determine early on that a career in cybersecurity is exciting for you, there are many ways to break into the industry. The first thing to do is to become educated. In high school, this may include talking to your guidance counselor to determine what courses are available to you that would provide a good foundation for a budding cybersecurity professional and then enrolling in those courses. Some high schools have cybersecurity programs like college majors where students complete specific courses that align with cybersecurity certifications. As a high school student, you can earn your certs. There may also be a cybersecurity club you can join. If there isn't a club in your school, you may want to consider starting one yourself and inviting other students to join. Also, look for "capture the flag" events sponsored by schools or community organizations. By taking high school courses, participating in clubs, and entering capture the flag events, you will quickly be on your way to a career in cybersecurity.

If you decide to continue your education at a college or university with a cybersecurity program, remember to check the statistics to determine if their students are getting ample internship and job opportunities. Again, reverse engineer the programs to ensure you pick a program whose students are quickly hired by organizations while in college and after graduation. In addition, you don't have to choose a major in cybersecurity to be successful, although it will help. Many large organizations have partnerships with universities. The organizations may provide the universities with resources in curriculum development, funding, and ultimately jobs for their students.

Career Transitioning

Many of us are transferring to cybersecurity from another career. Research shows that employees of organizations who were mainly already in an IT job filled the first cybersecurity jobs. These individuals were tapped or volunteered to help out with this effort. I don't think the early practitioners of cybersecurity believed that the talent shortage would be the way it is today.

I believe transitioning from your current job within your organization is the easiest way into a career in cybersecurity. Your organization's leaders already know that you're interested and might even see skills in you that are great for cybersecurity that you have not yet seen in yourself.

If you are attempting to transition from a job at one organization to a position in cybersecurity at a new organization, your work to break in will be more difficult. If you are taking this route, you will need to demonstrate how your current skills transfer to the new job. To do this, you should consider ways to obtain knowledge and experience on your own. You can get this knowledge by taking on stretch assignments at your current company, volunteering, self-study, obtaining certifications, or possibly completing a degree in cybersecurity. Seeking advice from someone who has taken this path will also be helpful as they will provide guidance, so you don't waste a lot of time and money.

Each path to breaking into the industry is challenging, but with clear direction and a focused strategy, you will be able to break in.

Resources:
- https://www.todaysmilitary.com/joining-eligibility/asvab-test
- https://www.army.mil/article/231249/new_entrance_test_to_increase_soldier_quality_reduce_attrition
- https://www.careeronestop.org/ExploreCareers/Assessments/self-assessments.aspx
- https://www.dol.gov/agencies/eta/onet/tools
- https://www.gallup.com/cliftonstrengths/en/strengthsfinder.aspx

Chapter 2 – Key Points and Recommended Actions

The following is a quick summary of the key points from this chapter:

- Think of your transition to cybersecurity as the first step in a journey that will have many stops along the way. Not only is this field new to you, but cybersecurity is a relatively new field that is still evolving.
- The value of research and planning cannot be overstated. Start by assessing your natural interests and strengths. Then read about the field and learn about the different disciplines within cybersecurity.
- Knowledge is power. After you have learned enough about the field to satisfy your initial curiosity, it's time to see where you stand. Assess your current skills against what you need to begin your transition, so you know where to start.
- Planning is key. Armed with a basic understanding of the field and an assessment of your skills, take the time to develop an action plan that addresses your first two positions in cybersecurity.
- Don't look at this as just a job. The most successful members of the cybersecurity community are focused on the mission. Embrace your passion.
- Get out there and talk to people. Talk to everyone you know who is in cybersecurity or who knows someone in cybersecurity. Remove the mystery. Know what you are getting into.

Chapter 3

Taking Inventory

Introduction

As we come to this third chapter, you have a better understanding of what a career in cybersecurity is like and have some methods and resources to help you decide where you might want to begin. This chapter is about how you can take stock of your skills, education, and experience, so you have a proper baseline to start building your career in cybersecurity.

Businesses today are highly connected via the Internet to technologies that enable commerce to be conducted globally in the blink of an eye. The complexity evident in the breadth of these technologies that are in use all over the planet and enmeshed in our daily lives can itself be daunting. The sole purpose of cybersecurity is to protect that highly complicated, critical worldwide network. As you can imagine, working in this field will require specific skills, education, and professional certifications. The purpose of this chapter is to provide you with some resources and methods to inventory what you already know and document what you don't yet know.

Understanding what you know is essential because it establishes your professional skill level at a current point in time. This inventory also helps you see just how much you don't know, which allows you to start building tools such as a career map documenting what skills or experience you may need for a future role.

This chapter is about getting to know yourself and being comfortable with the fact that you have much work to do to establish a career in cybersecurity. That's ok! We have all been there, and the essays that follow will show you that there are many resources available to get you started and processes you can use to document and focus on a specific career goal. So, roll up your sleeves, and let's get to work!

Improving Your Technical Skills and Key Resources ~ Gary

In the previous chapter, I explained how I got into IT but found my ultimate career in cybersecurity. I also discussed how I approached continual learning, which I think is essential for a career in this field.

This chapter focuses on taking inventory. We'll explore how you should look within yourself to see what you have and what you need to improve. It's going to be about us continuing our discussion on developing your career path. I will focus on websites and resources that you can use to educate yourself on new technologies or learn new skills required for employment. I will also discuss different websites and software tools I would recommend for improving your current skillsets and IT/cybersecurity knowledge. My goal in this chapter is to help you see the resources available to grow your career, develop your skills, and add to your experience.

By now you realize that I strongly believe that if you work in the field of cybersecurity, "continuous education" and "continuous improvement" should be your mantras. In cybersecurity, the technology, services, threats, vulnerabilities, and laws are constantly changing. Because this field encompasses many industries, you will need to understand that you can never know everything. However, that shouldn't stop you from educating yourself to be the elite cybersecurity professional you want to be. The point I want to make is that education doesn't stop. Stepping on this path is just the beginning.

From my LinkedIn article, "Path to a Career in Cyber and More,"[14] here is the "Cyber Career Path Workflow"[15] chart that I developed for our community. This workflow provides a view of how we would compare our skills/experience to those required for a particular

---

[14] https://www.linkedin.com/pulse/path-career-cyber-gary-hayslip-cissp-cisa-crisc-ccsk/
[15] https://app.box.com/Path-to-Cyber-slides

position and identify what we would need to accomplish if we wanted to qualify for that advertised job. I use this process today to keep my current career map up to date.

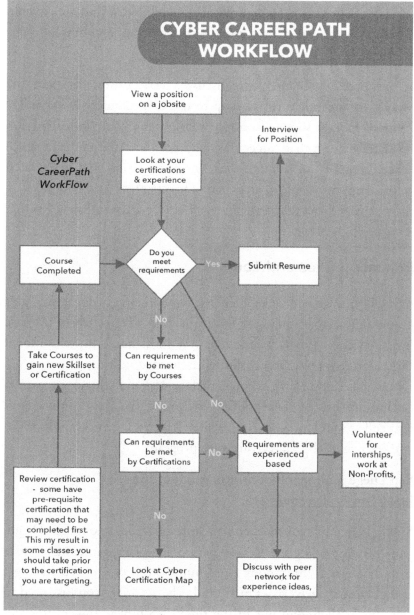

Figure 3.1 Cyber Career Path Workflow

As we start our discussion for this chapter, I want to note that two of the resources listed below are websites of programs located in San Diego, California. I use my home as an example to share with you the types of programs I recommend you look for in your area to help you begin your career, continue your education, and develop your career map.

In the previous chapter, we discussed certification lists and the process for creating a career map to use as a resource. Now we are going to look at some education websites and some tools that can help you mature that career map and get the skills and experience needed to apply for some of those interesting jobs. As I have stated before, I am by no means an expert. This chapter is based on my 20+ years of experience in the fields of IT and cybersecurity. With that said, let's have some fun!

Education Sites and Tools

As we begin, we will cover sites that contain either educational aids or useful tools that I have used over the years to re-certify or increase my knowledge of new technologies. We will start with educational sites. I am first going to list some sites located near my home in San Diego as examples of schools that you could attend to earn a certification or learn a new skill. I have found that many of these two-year colleges and four-year universities have adult education facilities with excellent labs and certification programs.

San Diego College of Continuing Education
http://www.sdce.edu/

SDCE is an adult education two-year program located in San Diego, and this school is great. I have personally taken numerous courses over the years at this school. I recommend this type of school to get free or close to free classes in IT and cybersecurity. You just need to sign up for them and put in the time to complete the courses and labs. This example has their programs grouped under the ICOM Academy at https://sdce.edu/icom, where they have programs for both IT and security, plus classes in Python. Using schools like these, you can be on your way into an entry-level position as you continue to develop your Cyber Career Map.

University of California San Diego Extension Program
http://extension.ucsd.edu/courses-and-programs

The University of California San Diego (UCSD) extension program's web page gives you access to all the certificate programs they have to offer. These courses cost money, but they are relatively cheap compared to paying for a college class in a degree program. Many colleges today offer extension courses or certifications, both online and in person. Check the universities in your area and see what courses or programs fit your career map. Hopefully, you will find some quality education and training to beef up a skillset you need for that future job.

Now let's move on to online resources that are not bound to any particular location.

Codeacademy
https://www.codcademy.com/

Codeacademy is one of many websites now available online where you can learn how to code. Some offer introductory classes for free with more in-depth services and courses for a fee. You will have to review them and decide if they fit your needs. What I like about this type of site is that you can do projects, and through that process, learn how to program in JavaScript, HTML/CSS, PHP, Python, or Ruby, and learn how to build APIs. Even though I work in cybersecurity, I still occasionally take classes in coding. Over my long career in IT and cybersecurity, I have found that being able to code often comes in handy, so don't neglect this part of your training.

Coursera
https://www.coursera.org/

Coursera is an excellent site for some free or low-cost training. The model is a little different in that you will need to buy your books.

There are also some available courses that you can count for college credit if you pay a fee. I have done classes in cybersecurity, cryptography, and mobile cloud apps. One school on this site, The University of Maryland, offers a group of courses that result in a cybersecurity certificate. I would recommend this site if you enjoy doing classes online at your own pace and don't mind the challenging curriculum. Just remember to keep up with your assignments and collaborate with your classmates.

Udemy
https://www.udemy.com/

Udemy is hands down one of the best training sites on the web. Courses on this site cost money, but for as low as $10, you can take a course in machine learning or coding in Python. I frequently use this site to learn new skills or because I am curious about a specific subject. I would highly recommend this site to you if learning in an online format works for you.

Pluralsight
https://www.pluralsight.com/

I keep an eye on Pluralsight as I have noticed they have IT Operations, Software Development, Creative Professional, and Business Development courses. This site is very similar to Udemy, except I find the courses more focused and grouped into specific career paths.

A Cloud Guru
https://acloudguru.com/

A Cloud Guru is well developed and covers the three major cloud platforms – AWS, GCP, and Azure. There is a cost associated with it, but I have found that if you need experience in the cloud and want to develop new skills, this site, with its trainers and curriculum, is outstanding.

Boson
https://www.boson.com/

Boson is an example of a resource focused on helping you prepare for passing specific IT/Cybersecurity certifications. Another reason I list them is that their network simulator software is one of the better tools out there that you can use to simulate building large networks without having to purchase hardware. Unfortunately, this costs some money, but I have used their product to prepare for numerous exams or simulate network designs before actually building them to ensure we had designed them correctly. Boson is an example of another resource you can use to learn network engineering and get experience building them. Just like Cloud Guru above, it's good to have a sandbox where you can create and break things, learn from your mistakes, and then reset and try again.

DDOS Protection Services
http://ddosattackprotection.org/blog/cyber-security-blogs/

Part of the process of developing as a security professional is staying informed. This link is to an article that lists the Top 100+ Cyber Security Blogs. I list it as a resource to help educate you on the various cybersecurity community professionals. I would recommend that you go through the blogs and sites listed in this article, bookmark several to start, and get into the habit of reading them weekly so you are informed of changes in your new community.

DistroWatch.com
http://distrowatch.com/

As you pursue a career in cybersecurity, you will probably find the need to learn the Linux operating system. This site has information about hundreds of different Linux distributions. This site is essential because if you want to gain experience, it's time to roll up your sleeves and start learning how to download and install your first Linux distribution. This site also has links to weekly newsletters and can keep you up to date on Linux. Just don't get overwhelmed. Pick a flavor of Linux like CentOS or Ubuntu that is mature and stable and enjoy!

The main thing to keep in mind is that you are starting on a path that will take time. Don't be afraid to put in the work to build the career you want. I would recommend that you approach this in increments, and over time you will be surprised at your progress.

Skills Assessment ~ Chris

Now that you have done the needed self-discovery to prepare for your transition into the cybersecurity industry, you have a general idea of where you want to go. The next step is to conduct a gap assessment between the skills needed for your desired roles and the skills you currently possess.

One type of analysis I like to use is the SWOT analysis. SWOT stands for strengths, weaknesses, opportunities, and threats. It's a strategic planning technique, but what could be more strategic than assessing your perfect job in cybersecurity?

To perform a SWOT analysis, you first need to think about your strengths and weaknesses relative to the particular role you are targeting. You may have identified this information in the self-discovery phase. If not, there is no time like the present. In addition to strengths and weaknesses, you'll need to identify the opportunities and threats. This process can be a little tricky because it isn't as straightforward as it would seem. For this part of the analysis, you must speculate about your opportunities and threats. You also may benefit from some additional research into the field. What you uncover could be excellent potential talking points during an interview.

Let's walk through an example. First, write down the pain points that were common themes in your informational interviews or research into the field. An example might be that security operation center (SOC) analysts often face alert fatigue. So how does this present an opportunity for you? Do you pick up technology easily? Do you have greater than average attention to detail? Can you focus on details for longer than the average person? Having the ability to identify these opportunities and thinking about possible solutions to them can help you stand out during an interview when there are multiple candidates for the job.

Thinking about threats is another helpful exercise. Certainly, you don't want to invest too much time into something which might soon be obsolete or replaced. Identifying these threats can help you focus on your career moves. For example, does automation help reduce alert fatigue by automating many of the repetitive tasks SOC analysts perform? If so, perhaps this is not a long-term role for you, but maybe you see yourself starting off doing the job and then being part of the automation team that helps bring innovation to the SOC function.

Below is an example of how a SWOT analysis might look.

Strengths	Weakness
- Analytical mindset - Ability to spot patterns - Learn new techniques quickly	- Dislike repetitive tasks - Not able to work 24/7 shifts (graveyard shifts particularly)
Opportunities	**Threats**
- Technology is evolving quickly - Increased demand for threat detection & analytics	- Automation is taking over this role - Candidates with previous security experience

Figure 3.2 Security Operations Center (SOC) Analyst SWOT Diagram

While thinking about the output of your SWOT analysis, you can use the sections below to either help highlight skills you might have skipped or add new skills that were previously missing.

Don't Forget about the Transferable Skills

After conducting informational interviews and research on particular roles that might interest to you, you will notice specific competencies or skills repeatedly highlighted as necessary. Your SWOT analysis will identify some of these skills, but some you may have missed.

Frequently, those who have not entered the market for a new job or have been in another industry might not see how some of the skills and competencies they possess align with the cybersecurity industry.

Look at what abilities and skills were required in jobs you've held in the past and how they might be like the requirements of a particular new cybersecurity role. As mentioned earlier, the NICE Cybersecurity Framework[16] has a great breakdown of tasks, skills, knowledge, and abilities. You can use these to look for similarities in your current or previous roles. For example, librarians are skilled in finding commonalities between different subjects and authors and looking for where they might find those resources. A salesperson might break down complex topics into simple-to-understand language to get their point across in a persuasive manner. Being able to research, analyze, draw conclusions, and provide suggestions are practical skills. You might already have transferable skills from your passions or previous work experiences that would be valuable in your next role.

As you can see, the gap between what is required and the skills you must acquire is often not as extensive as it seems at first.

Learning/Expanding on the Technical Skills

With your skills gap clearly in mind, it's time to start looking at how to close the gap. Here are some techniques that have been helpful to me. I'll describe these in detail in the pages that follow.

- Using a self-study approach
- Technical boot camps
- Studying for certifications
- Taking classes at a community college
- Obtaining a degree

---

[16] https://niccs.us-cert.gov/workforce-development/cyber-security-workforce-framework/

- Using a blended approach

Self-study

There are many options to consider, each with its pros and cons, but they are dependent on your learning style. For example, with self-study, think about whether you have the discipline to study on your own. The research would likely involve combining resources from websites, blogs, video blogs, and technical videos. This approach requires you to develop your own curriculum. The upside is that the curriculum can be customized to your specific passions and allow you to carve out a unique specialization for yourself.

> *Pro Tip: being able to differentiate yourself from others by having a specialization that is either limited or unique to the market and filling a need will lead to a greater chance of success.*

I recommend that you develop your curriculum with a checklist of all the things you want to learn and keep at it until you have accomplished them all. While this can evolve as you discover your passions or see technology changes that you wanted to master, try to keep the original and amend it with the changes. This checklist can also be used as a resource later in your career to help others or provide a story to future employers.

Boot Camps

Those who don't want to go down the theoretical route or already have a degree can consider technical boot camps like coding camps or boot camps geared towards completing a certification. There are pros and cons to these boot camps. What you get from these is up to you. Some will go into these with the sole purpose of passing a certification exam. However, I don't recommend this. If you just do these to pass the certification and don't truly learn the skills and competencies, you won't be able to dive into the topic during an interview or deliver on the job. As these boot camps are typically condensed into a couple of days or a week-long course, you might want to supplement this with outside resources like hands-on virtual labs or an in-home virtual lab to hone your skills. Conference training classes, frequently add-ons to many large industry conferences, are another excellent avenue for learning. Additionally, by combining them, you often do not have to add more time or travel expenses for a separate standalone class later.

Certifications

Certifications should be used to demonstrate that you understand the content covered by the certification. You can use certifications to provide you with the guidelines for a learning curriculum so that you can focus your learning on a particular area. For example, the CISSP certification focuses on eight different security domains[17] that encompass the field of cybersecurity.

- Security and Risk Management
- Asset Security
- Security Architecture and Engineering
- Communication and Network Security
- Identity and Access Management (IAM)
- Security Assessment and Testing
- Security Operations
- Software Development Security

These domains can help you focus your training and provide you with an industry-known standard body of knowledge. These exams are often broad and not particularly deep. This is by design so they can test for a reasonable level of knowledge about the topic. You do not have to limit yourself to the scope of the exam. If there is a

---

[17] https://www.isc2.org/Certifications/CISSP/Domain-Refresh-FAQ

particular area of interest, dive deep into it and learn as much as possible.

> *Suppose your goal is just to pass the certification exam and you do not truly understand the content. In that case, this lack of knowledge will come up during the interview process, or during the introductory or probation period of many jobs, so it is best to master the information.*

Traditional Education

Next, let's discuss utilizing traditional education opportunities to expand your knowledge, learn new skills, or develop additional competencies. Community or technical colleges have programs focused on expanding knowledge on a particular topic and allowing students to comprehend the subjects, typically within two years. Universities and four-year colleges expand on the topics. Usually, they add more rigor to the process, enabling students to have more in-depth theoretical experiences with analysis, research, writing, and knowledge around a subject. As technology evolves, colleges are slowly changing too. More and more colleges are starting to offer technical, hands-on experiences for their students. This hands-on curriculum is driven in part by feedback from the job market that graduates often don't have the hands-on technical experiences needed to be successful right out of the gate.

If you are considering this route, see if you can find schools with a hands-on technical approach. Keep in mind that it doesn't have to be on campus for this to happen. Ask about virtual labs, projects, internships, and if their professors are also practicing in the field and can share what the market needs. Some colleges are offering students courses geared towards some of the entry-level certifications, combining the curriculum with the ability to earn a certification. In the end, having these certifications and a degree will help set you apart from your peers.

You will note that many job descriptions still have four-year degree requirements for many entry-level roles. This is starting to shift as big companies like Google, Apple, EY, Deloitte, and others are beginning to remove degree requirements from their job descriptions. Other job sectors like work for the Government or as a Government contractor will likely not remove some of these degree requirements for a long time.

Blended Approach

Online courses offer a blend of traditional classes and self-study. You could complete some modules (for example, a YouTube explanation video) in as little as a couple of minutes. But it will take several hours for more in-depth courses and several months to approach the depth of traditional university classes. Some well-known universities provide courses for free or for a small fee. Some of these courses help you hone a particular skill or a specific tool. Some are full-blown university-style curriculums utilizing Massive Open Online Courses (MOOCs). Some platforms like MOOCs offer certificates of completion which allow you to demonstrate that you completed the course. You could use these to help you ramp up quickly on a particular skill, technology, or application, but be sure to supplement with hands-on/virtual practice sessions.

Additional Resources for Growth

There are many different types of resources that you can use to continue to expand your knowledge or continuously learn new topics or keep up with the ever-changing industry. The list below is my curated collection of additional resources:

- Books / Audiobooks – https://www.linkedin.com/pulse/my-collection-cybersecurity-books-christophe-foulon-cissp/
- Podcasts - https://www.linkedin.com/pulse/my-collection-cybersecurity-podcasts-christophe-foulon-cissp/

- Websites/Articles – https://www.linkedin.com/pulse/collection-security-feeds-christophe-foulon-cissp/
- Self-learning – https://www.linkedin.com/pulse/my-collection-cybersecurity-learning-platforms-foulon-cissp/
- Educational Platforms and Online Learning Communities – https://www.linkedin.com/pulse/my-collection-cybersecurity-learning-platforms-foulon-cissp/

Hiring Managers Also Do Assessments ~ Renee

Although there are non-technical components of a cybersecurity department, like security awareness and policy development and management, to name a few, many areas of the department include technical areas like network security or cloud security.

With many of the more technical roles being harder to fill, having technical skills will give you an additional boost when seeking to transition into cybersecurity. As previously shared, having technical skills isn't an ironclad requirement; however, it will make you a more desirable candidate. Many organizations are looking for technical expertise even when hiring for entry-level cybersecurity roles. In the paragraphs below are comments from cybersecurity leaders whom I interviewed in 2018. They shared their experiences about the technical skills that they look for when hiring. Some of the comments highlight skills they can develop in people they meet who are interested in breaking into the industry. Other anecdotes are about skills they obtained that made them more marketable when breaking into the industry. I think you'll find both perspectives helpful.

Technical skills training can start early – even in high school

As shared in a previous chapter, we can teach cybersecurity skills very early in life. For example, I discussed high school students who participated in a program where they learned cybersecurity skills and prepared for certifications. I make this point not because I believe most of you reading this book are in high school – although a few ambitious high schoolers may read the book. Instead, I make the point so that you know that anyone can learn technical skills to be successful in cybersecurity at any stage in their professional career.

When we chatted, Chris Huntington was the CISO at Nexigen and is now the CISO at FHLB in Cincinnati. Chris discussed a program where he works with high school students and trains them on technical skills. These are the types of skills that he would want a person new to cybersecurity to have and that would be helpful for them to have early in their cybersecurity careers. "We're doing a program here called Tech Defenders, which starts in high school. So, going all the way back to freshman year of high school, we're hitting them with information security. We're hitting them with best practices and how to do networking, and how to set up servers. [We want to provide] them with a technical perspective early on."

Taking cybersecurity courses or getting a degree is an option

To completely transition to a new career, Candice Camp, now the Head of Insider Threat at GE, decided to go back to school for a network security degree to help her better understand technology and security. This degree program helped complement her theatre degree with technical skills.

Candice was a theatre major before she decided to go back and get a network security degree. "I started looking around at different programs that schools were offering and looked at the IT programs. IT looked interesting. I wasn't sure what my aptitude would be at that point, but I decided to give it a try. A network security degree sounded like it would be really interesting and future-looking, so that's what I did. I realized that I had a strong aptitude for it. I got to do a lot of cool things, like coding, and learning all the different security toolsets that are used by incident handlers. I came out of there with a job offer immediately as an information security analyst at a small company. I then was able to do a huge variety of different pieces of security because it was a smaller team."

Anthony Dupree, former CISO and CIO of CareerBuilder, spoke of a 50-question fill-in-the-blank technical test to vet a candidate's technical skills. He describes some of the conversations he has had with people about breaking into cybersecurity. "I've talked to people wanting to get into security. The first thing I ask them is, "Do you know what port DNS runs on? What is TCP vs. UDP? What port does it run? Do you know anything about the difference between a stateful and a stateless firewall?" Anthony required candidates to take his 50-question exam, and complete it in an hour: no multiple-choice, all fill-in-the-blank.

The goal of the examination is not for them to finish it. The goal is to see how thoughtful the candidate is. How thoughtful are the answers to the questions? In other words, if you have a fill-in, either you know it or you don't. If you know it, you will put down enough comments to let the prospective employer know you understand the basics.

That stops many folks from coming in. It forces them to say, "Well, I'm not ready for this role because these are the things. These are the attributes that I need to have to serve in that role. Because if you don't know the basics, then the higher-level responsibilities or technical requirements that you [need to perform] as an analyst, you won't be able to do it."

Anthony's test shows the interview strategies that some CISOs use. It illustrates that some CISOs really value technical skills and as a budding security professional, learning technical skills is a plus.

In conclusion, having technical skills provides you with so many opportunities when coming into security. More often than not, the roles seeking technical skills receive fewer applications, and the candidates who apply are more in demand. Therefore, by building up your technical skills, you will definitely have more security opportunities presented to you.

Chapter 3 – Key Points and Recommended Actions

The following is a quick summary of the key points from this chapter:

- The cybersecurity field requires a mindset of continual learning and continuous assessment and reassessment of your skills and the skills necessary for your next job and your next job after that.
- Your assessment and action plan should start well before you decide to apply for any position. You need to honestly assess what skills you have and what the job requires.
- There is an abundance of resources to acquire the skills you need. The key is continual assessment and continual learning.
- Your learning plan will include training, online courses, conferences, preparing for and obtaining certifications, and possibly even a degree.
- Use your network and do all the information interviews you can arrange. Look for the confluence of required skills to prioritize where you need to improve.
- Always be thinking two or three jobs ahead. Competence in specific cybersecurity capabilities can take years to attain, so be thinking years in advance.

Chapter 4

Soft Skills

Introduction

In IT and cybersecurity, the employees and coworkers who stand out are not those who have unbelievable technical skills but those who have mature soft skills. By definition, soft skills are a combination of social skills, communication skills, and personality traits that enable people to work well with others to achieve their goals. Many top performers who lead security teams are people with well-developed soft skills who can effectively communicate and be trusted to manage projects with little to no supervision.

We highlight this because we assume you are reading this book to enter a very technical career field, and we want you to know there are other skills that are just as important as whether you can code, configure a firewall, or reload an operating system. Cybersecurity is a team sport, and you will work closely with people who have different backgrounds, bring unique gifts, and have novel approaches to problem-solving. Sometimes this causes friction. This friction is why soft skills are essential, and they are something that you can learn and continuously improve as you develop in your career.

This chapter provides the viewpoints of three different cybersecurity professionals with extensive experience in working with both small and large teams and cutting-edge technologies. Notice how each of us views soft skills a bit differently and highlights different ones. This difference is significant because specific soft skills may be needed when you are entry-level, but as you travel down your career path and accept new roles and responsibilities, you will find that new soft skills will be required. The one central point we want you to take from this chapter is that continuously nurturing your soft skills is just as crucial for your career as being a lifelong technical learner.

Cyber Soft Skills and Then Some ~ Gary

In today's business environment, it is generally accepted that there is a cybersecurity talent shortage. There are more jobs than applicants, and those who apply are missing fundamental skills, education, certifications, and experience. One of the complaints I hear from many people is that the applicants they are hiring are also missing specific soft skills, which I think many of us who have been in the industry for years take for granted. These skills are different from technical skills such as mobile security, data analytics, security analysis, or software code development.

The skills I am talking about are essential skills that we expect our employees to have to work together effectively. As we begin this chapter, let me paint for you a picture of how this issue was highlighted for me as I attended an event in San Diego for high school students thinking about technology career fields. This event allowed students to meet professionals in various career fields, and one of the questions they were required to ask is, "What soft skills do you feel are required for me to be successful in <your> career field." I have to admit that the kids definitely got me thinking with that question. I spent most of the afternoon after the event thinking, "What soft skills do I think help make one successful in the field of cybersecurity?"

Understand there are many skills we expect professionals in our field to have when they come to work. Maybe we take for granted that you will have them already, but that is the focus of this chapter. I'd like you to think about what soft skills you have that would benefit a potential employer and make sure you not only list them on your résumé but speak about them during your interview. So, with that in mind, here are five core soft skills I feel are essential to professionals in the cybersecurity career field:

1. *Curiosity and Problem-Solving* – The technology and threats in cyber are rapidly evolving, and I feel curiosity is an asset

for someone who works in this field. It is why people hack; it is why people innovate; it's why we get creative in developing new solutions to a problem after troubleshooting for three days straight. It's the fascination for how technology works, how it can be broken, and how it can be rearranged to do things no one imagined.

2. *Responsibility and Accountability* – In IT and cybersecurity, you break things. You have projects that can have tremendous impacts on an organization – both good and bad. In situations like these I look to see who steps up, takes the lead in projects, and owns it if it goes bad. In cybersecurity, much of your experience is from projects, integrating new technologies, troubleshooting issues, and you need to be accountable for your actions and responsible to your team and organization to deliver what you promise.

3. *Communication* – In cybersecurity, you will never know everything; you will at times have to request information or assistance. It is essential that you can be adaptable and collaborate with people. The key to doing this is that you must be able to communicate effectively. Whether it's through discussions, written reports, or presentations, having the ability to listen, take notes, understand another point of view, and get your point across without being condescending is critical.

4. *Teamwork* – In cybersecurity, you work in teams, so the question is, are you able to keep the team goals in mind when working to deadlines and work with your teammates to achieve them? Here I am interested to see if, as you work in a team, you can be honest, offer constructive criticism when required, and listen to others in completing the assigned deadlines. There will be times in your career in cybersecurity

where you may be an individual contributor, where you are a lone researcher. Whatever the case, you still work for a larger organization and will be part of some team, so it's crucial to work with other people and be trusted to get your assignments done and provide value to the team.

5. *Time Management* – Finally, in cybersecurity, we often deal with multiple issues at the same time. You must organize what information you have and prioritize it to focus your time and resources on what is essential to the team and business. I think this is essential for working in this dynamic career field. In almost 30 years of working in this industry, I can't think of one time when time management was not crucial in managing issues.

These are my five essential soft skills for you to succeed in your new cybersecurity career. I am sure many of you may have different opinions. What is crucial, though, as you start your career path in our community is to understand that technical skills will only get you so far. Soft skills will enable you to excel in leadership positions and will provide you with many options and a lengthy career in cyber. Good luck!

Don't Forget About the Soft Skills ~ Chris

There has been a massive shift to technology and technology-native businesses within the past decade. This shift requires a trained workforce for support and security. With the increased demand for a technology-focused workforce, candidates are flocking to technology-related jobs, especially those in the cybersecurity field.

Often, candidates will focus only on the technical skills and forget about the soft skills, but the soft skills are critical for your long-term growth and success. Job descriptions focus on the technical requirements of the roles. But hiring managers that I have spoken to and interviewed on my podcast, "Breaking into Cybersecurity," state that they would train candidates on the needed technical skills if they had the required soft skills to succeed in the role. My goal in this chapter will be to highlight those highly sought-after soft skills requested by hiring managers to provide you with the opportunity to learn and hone those skills and be able to demonstrate them to hiring managers during your job search.

Based on my interviews on "Breaking into Cybersecurity," the most commonly requested soft skills (ranked in order of importance) are:

1. Communication / Writing Skills
2. Curiosity / Research
3. Collaboration and Teamwork
4. Problem-solving / Analytical thinking
5. Adaptability
6. Attention to details

I want to focus on the **top three** of those skills and show how the listed skills interact. Some of these skills have sub-components that coincide with the others, and growth in one of these areas can have ripple effects across multiple skills.

Communication

The ability to communicate effectively is the number one soft skill requested by hiring managers. This skill, particularly, seems to be a challenge in the cybersecurity field because security engineers are better known for interacting with computers behind the scenes than with people. Social interactions and communication are critical in cybersecurity because a vital objective of this field is to help the business achieve its business outcomes through secure operations. The first step is to sit down with different stakeholders to understand their mission and how they achieve their objectives. Additionally, they should be able to converse with stakeholders who have various technical knowledge levels to know what they need and how to help them.

A key sub-skill for effective communication with the business is asking probing questions to achieve a deeper understanding and see things from the stakeholder's point of view. Then practitioners need to think analytically about the business's problems. The ability to research the problem and develop a solution that enables the company to be successful and minimizes its risk is critical to bringing about behavioral change. Your chance of being successful is further enhanced by effectively communicating your recommendations in both written and verbal forms.

As you can see, the ability to communicate with the business encompasses several different skills that you will need to master.

Curiosity

Curiosity is another soft skill that is fundamental for success in cybersecurity. Often cybersecurity practitioners are brought in to solve problems that cross multiple domains such as technology, legal, compliance, and risk. Hiring managers are looking for candidates that are curious enough to get to the root cause of problems to solve them. To deliver on this requirement, candidates must demonstrate that they are open to discovery and figuring out how things work to develop solutions to their company's problems.

Another aspect of being curious is that you find ways to learn continuously, which can fuel your passion for the field. Continuous learning and development are essential ways to drive growth in this industry, but you need to do so in a way that grows your passions and makes you happy while not stressing you out. Broaden your horizons. Lessons learned from other disciplines can translate to cybersecurity. The ability to think outside the box and apply lessons learned from different fields to create innovative solutions will help you stand apart from others.

Collaboration

The third commonly requested soft skill I'd like to cover is collaborating well with others. The ability to collaborate with others means that you can work with them to deliver on a common goal. You can collaborate within a traditional team structure or just by working closely together towards completing a common goal without any formal system. Cybersecurity professionals are expected to collaborate with different business units or other teams within their departments, which requires them to be adaptable to the changing situations or different ways of interacting with outside groups. Teamwork is also a skill closely associated with collaboration. Cybersecurity professionals are often required to be part of ad-hoc teams to complete a project or respond to a security incident. Being in an ad-hoc team requires them to quickly adapt to the communication and working styles of the different team members.

As you can see, the soft skill of collaboration is also a combination of skills that includes adaptability, problem-solving, and teamwork. Combining these allows cybersecurity professionals to work with others and effectively deliver on their assigned business objectives.

Soft Skills in Practice ~ Renee

One of my favorite questions to ask cybersecurity leaders is if they've transitioned someone without technical skills into security. As I've said, most people in this industry have transitioned from another area of technology or another business area. There are relatively few people starting their careers in security. This chapter shares some quotes directly from security leaders who hired people early in their security careers based mostly on their soft skills. These stories will give you hope that you don't have to be the most technical person to get a cybersecurity job.

I mentioned Chris Huntington in the previous chapter, and he also talked about culture fit when looking for people to join his organization. "We see this is the right person when they fit our culture first. Even if they meet or exceed our technical requirements, if they are not going to fit in our culture, I can't train them. When we see that talent, we grab them fast. We don't let them go to the competition. We don't want them to go to somebody else."

In the last chapter, we also discussed Candice Camp, a security leader who was a theatre major and went back to school for a network security degree. Why did she decide to go back to school? She thought she could use her creative, investigative thinking. "It just sounded more interesting. It sounded like I could use more of my creative, investigative thinking, not necessarily the math involved in the coding side of computer science. I didn't have that background. There were [a lot of] programs popping up at that time that were security-focused in the early 2000's, so it was the exciting thing to do back then."

Amy Bogac described the soft skills that she had that made her realize that security was a good fit. "I love figuring out puzzles. I didn't like solving a problem by resetting a router or rebooting a server. I wanted to understand why the way that the technology was supposed to work wasn't working. That is how I built my brand in IT, was able to be what I refer to ... as the human event correlation engine. I can see patterns and obscure points of connectivity, and I was never really satisfied with any project I was working on until the root cause of the root cause was clearly identified and resolved."

Anthony Dupree shared his thoughts on people who didn't have the passion for the role and how that impacts his view of them when hiring. "One of the things I discovered was many people wanted to be in security, but they didn't have the passion. They didn't have the passion because they were in this bubble. They were insulated in what they were doing, and they weren't looking outward.

Security is about outward. You have to have an outward-looking approach. The bad guys are looking at the next best thing to get into your organization...whether they use something from 20 years ago or use cutting edge technologies like AI or gamification.

The question for us is [that] you have to have something like an entrepreneurial, innovative spirit in security. You can't just look at the obvious. You've got to look at what's behind the obvious because if you're experiencing a DDOS attack, and it's odd that you're being DDOS'd, it may be coming through a backdoor. That's another camouflage attack they're trying to use to steal from your organization.

I think that for me, it is really about how to take that talent, give them the broad view, give them the tools so that they can do great things."

Adam Hirsch describes hiring entry-level team members from the office services/mailroom department because of their soft skills.

"They're coming in from the mailroom, and they don't have any IT background. They may have some technical acumen, but we look for people who are more motivated and want to progress [in] their careers and are generally interested in security. Not just the money – but they're interested in it as a profession, a career.

We're doing similar with college students, those who are interns. We'll bring them in, train them up just to learn our secrets and processes to get them moving, but I've always been a big proponent of having everyone get a professional development plan. What [do] they want to be doing next? Whatever their career is hopefully in security, what that career is because a lot of different [?] then go over the training plan around that.

What skills do you need to get to your five-year plan, and then from that work perspective, what technical skill or soft skill training programs can you receive from your employer? Build that plan out, and then what are the personal development training they're going to take, whether reading a book, attending webinars, or obtaining certifications. Everyone has to revisit their training plans for the year, and then at the beginning of the year, they identify what training they want to take, schedule that."

Soft Skills Mismatch

Knowing yourself is vital because your soft skills may not be the right fit for specific cybersecurity roles. Carla Donev, who came from an accounting and audit background, shared a story of someone who had a mismatch of soft skills for her security manager role. She recruited someone from the internal audit department because she needed an excellent administration professional and manager to lead the team. He struggled because he was too focused on the technology and didn't think he was a fit. When she asked him how he felt when there was a breach, he said he got really nervous when there was an incident and wanted to hide under the covers. They both concluded that the role wasn't for him.

In conclusion, being aware of and honing your soft skills is very important if you want to join a cybersecurity team or any working team. Being able to leverage your most essential soft skills and strengthen them is crucial for being a desirable candidate for a cybersecurity role.

Chapter 4 – Key Points and Recommended Actions

The following is a quick summary of the key points from this chapter:

- Even though many disciplines within cybersecurity are very technical, soft skills are essential for success.
- Chief among the highly valued soft skills are "fit for culture" skills such as collaboration, teamwork, communication, and adaptability.
- Given the sheer pace of many cybersecurity departments, "reliability" predictors such as time management, accountability, and attention to detail are critical.
- Fit for culture and reliability is not enough. They must be augmented by your passion, curiosity, problem-solving, and analytical skills
- Reread Renee's last section of Chapter 1 and use one of the assessment tools if you haven't already. Focus on soft skills and focus on both what you excel at and what you need to shore up.

Section 3

Your Human Network

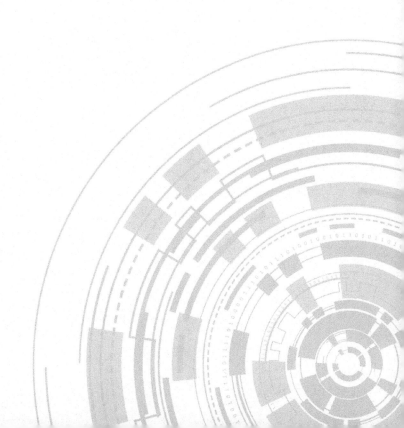

Introduction

In this section, we're going to explore two sides of the same coin. One side of that coin has been familiar to us for as far back as our collective memories go. The other is of relatively recent origin, going back barely a generation or two.

We have long understood the value of our personal network, what we call the human network. Because it is omnipresent in our lives, it is easy to overlook. But like a garden, it will either grow and flower for our benefit or be overrun and tangled, becoming useless to us.

If we tend to our network, we'll make sure it includes mentors, colleagues, former bosses, former employees, peers in other industries, recruiters, and people with whom we simply like to spend time.

Social media, when used properly, is the ultimate marriage of technology and the human network. However, given the magnifying power of using social media to ask a question, state a position, or make a connection, we need to be even more careful to tend this part of the garden well.

What we'll focus on in the following two chapters is how to build and maintain your personal human network. As with so much of our advice in this book, we start with planning and research. We believe you will get the most benefit from your actions if you target your activities based on what you want to accomplish in your career. We'll help you identify the specific groups in cybersecurity, and we'll help you really understand the mechanics of social media to remove the mystery if you're new to LinkedIn, Twitter, and the like.

We've often made the point that cybersecurity doesn't happen in a vacuum; it's a team sport. Your human network is your team.

Chapter 5

Your Network and the Cyber Community

Introduction

Community is defined as a social unit, a group of people with attributes in common such as norms, religion, values, customs, or identity. Communities are the next step. These are groups of people who share a sense of place, whether geographical or virtual. We share these definitions because it's essential for you to begin your cybersecurity career understanding that it's both a career and a very vibrant community. As you develop your career path, it's essential to develop a network of friends and peers.

Your network is more than just friends or followers you have on social media. Your network, as an example, should contain people you work with (peers in your field) and people you admire who could be possible mentors. It can also include friends, people from church, people who like the same hobbies as you; basically, it should be diverse. These should be people you have something in common with, and it helps if they like you. When we need help with an issue, when we need to ask a peer for advice, when we need to find a new job <grin>, that's right, we reach out to our networks. The reason it's essential is that each person in your network has a network of their own so think of it like skipping a stone across the surface of a still pond. After the rock hits the water, the ripples that cascade are like the people in your network responding to help you or direct you to someone who may need your assistance.

The focus of this chapter and our discussions is how to begin this process. Like most people, you probably already have friends and family. The next step is to build on this initial community and develop a new group that will mature into your career network. It is critical to understand that this career network you create will reflect your professionalism in our cybersecurity community. It's ok to grow it slowly, ask peers for advice and add people from diverse backgrounds. Remember, this will take time, so enjoy the discussions that follow, and let's begin your network journey.

Maturing Your Career Map and Joining Our Community – A Plan for Success! ~ Gary

I described in Chapter 2 how I found my career in cybersecurity and used the lab in my garage to develop my first career map. Then in Chapter 3, I described how resources like education sites, tools, and security blogs could help improve your inventory of skills and experience. In this chapter, I will tie it all together and provide one final resource that you can use to manage your career map and track the experience, certifications, or skills required for future employment.

For the sake of this discussion, I am going to talk about websites and resources I would use to track changes to a specific job type in the cybersecurity career field. The example we will use is: What are some new skills or experiences senior cyber security engineer positions are requiring for the candidates who apply for them? I will also add some information about joining professional organizations and why membership in peer groups is essential to building a professional peer network. As we begin, I want to remind you again that working in cybersecurity is dynamic. Change is the one constant you can expect. Therefore, continuous learning is a must to manage the change and avoid an impact on your career. You need to constantly be educating yourself because if you don't, this field will move right by you and leave you behind in the blink of an eye. Remember, once you start down this path, embrace continuous learning to have a vibrant, successful career.

As a refresher, the Cyber Career Map (see below) from Chapter 2 consists of a step-by-step career position tree that notes what certifications and experience would be required to work at a specific skill level. We will use it as a reference throughout our discussion in this chapter. Please note that some of the professional organization websites I use as examples are in San Diego, California. I only use them as an example to share the types of websites and organizations you should look for in your area.

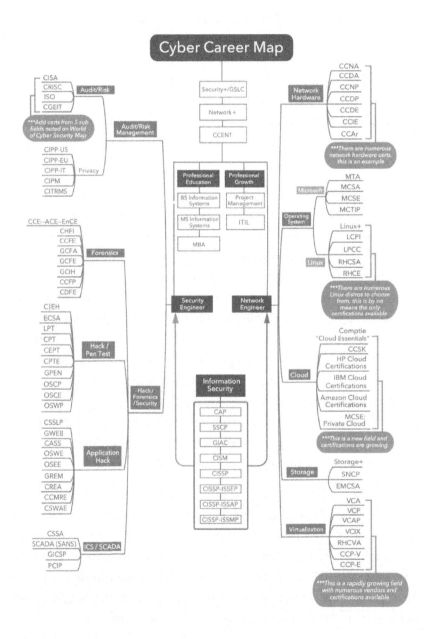

Employment Research and Networking Ideas

This section will cover websites I use to research positions, required skill sets and experience requirements for specific jobs or new career paths. As we finish this section, I will also include several professional organizations as examples of peer groups that you can join. This is essential to building your network and getting involved in our community.

Career Sites

LinkedIn (www.linkedin.com)

If you don't have a profile here, you are seriously hamstringing yourself. Just understand that this is not Facebook. LinkedIn is a professional site for career-minded individuals. I would recommend you set up your profile with a good picture, get active in your selected forums, and use it as a foundation to start building your professional network. A tool you will like on LinkedIn is the "Jobs" tab. Another thing I like about this website is that if you read people's profiles, you will see some very well-worded descriptions of work, projects, and experience that will assist you when you get stuck writing your résumé. I don't advocate copying someone else's profile, but it helps to view how others describe a difficult project or job experience.

Indeed (www.indeed.com)

Indeed.com is the number one job site in the world. The indeed.com website, therefore, has an extensive listing of open positions. I periodically review this site for roles that I find interesting. I like to compare the same type of position at different companies or in various locations to see how the requirements change or note how the compensation varies. Indeed.com provides insight into the skills and experience you should focus on as you develop your career and target a new job role. Using a site like this, you can take five to ten descriptions of a position, like Senior Security Engineer, and compare them. You will see that about 70% of the required skill sets, experience, and certifications are the same. You can use this information to fine-tune your career map and focus on those skill sets and certifications that are common, which will help you apply for more positions. The other 30% will be unique to the company or the specific role and how it fits the organization. Brainstorm with your network to discuss which of the 30% of unique requirements are essential and add them to your career plan.

Glassdoor (www.glassdoor.com)

Glassdoor began as an aggregator of anonymous company reviews from current and former employees. They have expanded to include pay information, interview styles, and most recently, job listings. I like to go to this site and put in a zip code, then put "Information Security" in the search field and review the jobs that pop up. Even at my career level today, I am still curious to see what companies in my area are hiring, what they are paying for talent, and what skill sets and certifications they expect a new hire to possess. I would recommend that you use a website like this and search in your area, looking at the types of positions you currently qualify for and then look for something that you would like to do in the future. With the "future" job listing, look at the position's requirements and then cross-check your career map and note your current location on the skill tree and what you would still need to complete if you wanted this future job. This continuous review provides you a goal to strive for while still working at your current job.

These three sites, taken together, give you an excellent research tool. You can use LinkedIn to get to know the people who form your peer group and the skills your peers think are important based on how they construct their profiles. You can use LinkedIn and Indeed to discover who is hiring and for what positions. You can use LinkedIn and Glassdoor to conduct extensive research about the companies you are targeting.

Now let's look at professional organizations and networking groups. I am sure there are many to choose from in your area, and I will discuss some in the San Diego area as examples of groups that I would recommend you check out and potentially get involved. I joined many of these organizations to discover the roles companies were hiring for in my area.

The following organizations also have regional, national, and in some cases, international affiliations. I'm relating my experience as a member of the local chapter and you can likely expect a similar setup in your region.

Professional Groups

Information Systems Security Association International (ISSA)
Parent website: www.issa.org
San Diego website: www.sdissa.org

ISSA is a nonprofit organization for the information security profession committed to promoting effective cybersecurity on a global basis. I have been a member of the San Diego chapter of ISSA for over ten years. They typically have monthly luncheons with speakers. I always try to go to these luncheons when my schedule permits. I even present at the San Diego chapter on occasion. The main thing to remember here is if you are starting in IT or cybersecurity, you will meet many people in both fields at these gatherings. It is here that you can collect information to fine-tune your cyber career map, and you can find mentors and grow your network.

Information Systems Audit and Controls Association (ISACA)
Parent website: www.isaca.org
San Diego website: www.isaca-sd.org

If you are into Network Auditing and Risk Management, this organization is for you. I have found that they have great presentations at the monthly meetings. Many of these presentations feature very knowledgeable people within the field of IT and cybersecurity. ISACA is an excellent organization to get involved with if there is a chapter in your area, and I would highly recommend it.

InfraGard
Parent website: www.infragard.org
San Diego website: www.infragardsd.org

This organization was established in 1996 as part of the InfraGard program. InfraGard is a partnership between the FBI and members of the private sector. The program provides a vehicle for seamless public-private collaboration with the government relevant to Critical Infrastructure protection. Membership comprises individuals representing private businesses, local, state, and federal law enforcement agencies, academic institutions, and first responders. The chapter consists of various sectors, from IT/Telecommunications to Emergency Services. There are 17 sectors in all. Each sector has monthly meetings, and the chapter sponsors region-wide events. An added value of this organization is it allows you to be involved in both the cybersecurity community and the larger regional community where you live.

Networking Groups

These are San Diego groups that I interact with regularly. I'm listing them here so you get a flavor for the kind of local groups I seek out. I'm listing them by their website address because that's how most of us conduct our searches.

http://sdtechscene.org/ – This is an event calendar of many local tech-oriented groups. It lists things happening daily in the San Diego area. Note that this site is managed by the San Diego Tech Scene, a local tech entrepreneurial organization, so it lists tons of stuff for tech startups. I go to many of the events to network and see new types of technologies.

Another site linked to them that is tied into the tech scene is **https://startupsd.org/**. The reason I go to startup events is to stay fresh with what is going on in technology. You may think this is not related to cybersecurity, but you would be wrong. Many new technologies turn into tomorrow's zero-day. Educate yourself, enjoy the community, network, and see some really cool tech. What's important here is to look for organizations or events like this in your area to grow your knowledge of your chosen career field and to grow your network.

http://evonexus.org/ – This website is linked to EvoNexus, an incubator for some incredible technology companies located in San Diego. Again, just like the SD Tech Scene, I go to the EvoNexus events to see how people are using technology. I am fascinated to see what entrepreneurs create and the hard work they and their teams go through to bring technology to market. As you create your career path, I would suggest you go to events like these in your area to see how quickly technology is evolving. Incubators remind us of the need to continually educate ourselves or get left behind, especially in Cybersecurity.

http://www.meetup.com/ – Right now, there are thousands of meetups here in San Diego going on all the time, and all you need to do is set up an account and start searching for groups that are meeting on things that you find interesting. It can be groups for professional networking, IT/Tech events, specific subjects like hacking, big data, drones, and bitcoin. Once you start looking at this site, you will see there are tons of things you can do. Make sure when you go to these events you have fun, educate yourself, and don't forget to bring your business cards with you.

I think it is important to state that you should use the tools available to you. With that in mind, I have included the diagram from Chapter

3 to remind you how to incorporate these sites into your process for updating your cyber career map.

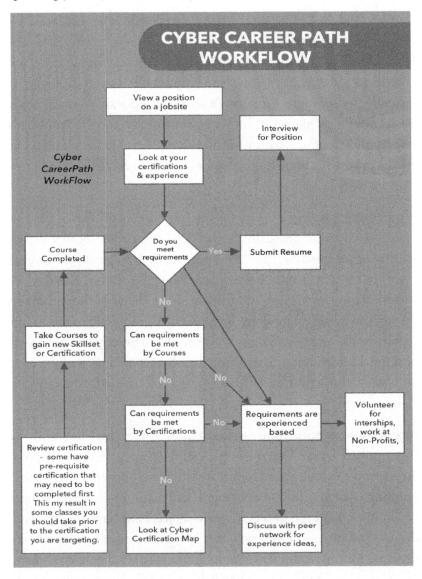

As always, I hope the information in this chapter will help you build the network you will need as you progress in your career, and some of the sites will help fine-tune your career map to meet current role requirements.

Why Growing a Network Is Important ~ Chris

Networking with people in a new or existing industry can lead to incredible benefits. Some of these benefits are meeting new people and making lifelong connections, finding mentors who can guide and influence your career, or even those willing to help you by introducing you to peers or employers who might need skilled employees like you. In this chapter I will share some of the tips that have helped me and others in their "people networking" journey.

While there are many cybersecurity positions that are going unfilled, the opposite is often the case for entry-level positions. Many people would like to develop a career in cybersecurity, and because of the ensuing rush to get into the cybersecurity industry, some companies could get anywhere from fifty to one hundred applications for every job posted. An analogy I like is the real estate market. When there is an abundant supply of inventory on the market, it becomes a "buyer's market," meaning the buyers can better control the deal's terms and sellers are more apt to give concessions. The employment market, especially during depressed times, becomes such a market because there are more candidates on the market than roles available, making the employers more dominant in the decision-making process.

Recruiters are sometimes overloaded in such a buyer's market due to numerous applicants for the limited number of positions. Therefore, I am sharing the information below to provide insights on some of the tools they might use to help them manage candidate flow.

- Phantom listing – A "phantom listing" is a job post without a particular position being available within the organization, the purpose of which is to collect résumés and create profiles of prospective candidates to reach out to later when a role might open. Recruiters also keep listings up until the selected candidate starts, in case something happens, and the preferred candidate doesn't fill the position.

- Evergreen requisition – Companies use an "evergreen requisition" for a position the company always needs to fill, particularly for high-turnover jobs. Sometimes these positions appear to have gone unfilled for months. If you spot one of these positions, rather than wonder why it's so hard for this company to fill the role, consider applying. They may bring in lots of candidates to consider for this role, and you might score what amounts to at least an informational interview if you turn out not to be qualified.
- Stalking horse – Sometimes, a company might open a role and post it publicly when they already have almost certainly determined that the position will go to an internal candidate. They do so to ensure that they are going with the best resource on the market.
- Unpublished position – Before the public recruiting process begins, positions are proposed internally to obtain a budget and define the role's responsibilities.

The goal of networking is to minimize the effect of these techniques in slowing down your search. Having a network of individuals throughout the industry who can help you is a powerful tool when conducting a job search. Over time, you help each other, form new connections, introduce each other, collaborate on technical problems, or even just socialize. Then, when it comes time for your job search, your network can help you bypass office politics, see through the phantom and stalking horse listings, and hopefully, uncover the unposted jobs. Once a connection of yours surfaces an unposted job opportunity, they can often access people within the company who might speak directly to the hiring managers' recruiters and share your profile instantly.

With so many different ways to meet new people, you might be thinking to yourself, which is the best? Like my response to the question of "How do you get into cybersecurity?" the answer to the question is, "That depends." Are you comfortable walking up to new people and introducing yourself to them in person? Do you prefer ensuring that there is at least a mutual sense of commonality before introducing yourself? Would you rather interact with people online before meeting them? There are pros and cons to each approach, and it's up to you and the situation which one makes the most sense for you.

To start tapping into the underground job market, you need to start building out your network. This network can be a combination of online, in-person, or even second degree connections introduced through your growing personal network. I recommend you start by ensuring that you have a LinkedIn profile (more to come on social media in Chapter 6) and start building your network with people you know, including former coworkers and friends.

Let's start with building your network online, as it is likely the easiest to get started on and can become the foundation for the rest. Whether online or offline, you can begin to expand your network by reaching out to people who might be in the company, job role, or niche of cybersecurity that interests you. Start by introducing yourself, share why you reached out, and strike up a virtual conversation. The idea is that you want to get to know the person genuinely, and they should get to know you as well; if not, these are superficial connections and usually end up not being more than acquaintances. Here are some tips:

- Don't use your first connection to ask if they are hiring. How would you like it if the first thing that someone did when people introduced themselves to you was to try to sell you something or ask for a favor? You probably would not like it, and this is how they might feel as well.
- Ask for advice to help you with something within their expertise that is not related to introducing you to someone else, providing a referral to their company, or looking at your résumé. Start with something small, and maybe show that

you have attempted to tackle the problem already and share the results. Asking for advice acknowledges that they have a level of expertise and people generally like to help when they feel they have something to contribute.
- Aim to build a relationship first, share your goals, your interests, and the rest shall come. Then, after a level of trust is developed, you might ask for a more considerable favor or assistance to refer you, introduce you, or connect you to someone related to the company or role you are targeting.
- Don't approach this as a transaction, moving each new contact from stage to stage, softening them up for the big ask. Instead, invest in your people network over time and come at this from the perspective that you want to give more than you take. Your network will be of more value to you, and you'll likely feel better about giving than taking.

Ways to grow your virtual network

The cybersecurity community has many other social media channels in addition to LinkedIn, Twitter, and Facebook. These are typically found on Slack and Discord and offer more specialized networks or groups for individuals to join. Many of them are "by invitation," indicating you need to establish trust first. While links to many of these "by invitation" groups are harder to find on your own, dialoguing with people you meet will eventually uncover them. Open Meetups and Slack groups are a great place to start. You can use these methods to grow your network, meet people in the industry, and get to know your peers. You just need to pick the virtual "places" you feel most comfortable and establish a presence.

Unless you live in a rural area, or there is a global pandemic affecting your ability to network, go to career fairs, conferences, and in-person meetups. You might be thinking about how you can rise above other candidates and appeal directly to hiring managers or recruiters. Social media, virtual happy hours, and virtual career fairs may seem to replace these events, but they are not the same. Virtual events do not spark the same kind of connection you get when you meet someone in person. For hiring managers, it's much easier to spot what they are looking for in a candidate.

General networking things you should always be doing

If you are very social, there might be places where individuals in certain professions in your areas are known to gather (like a favorite restaurant or bar) or *Meetups* in those same areas of groups that might share a similar interest. I know of several of these groups in the Washington DC area who meet at different restaurants around the city every third Wednesday of the month. Usually, this information is posted on their *Meetups* page for members and as an incentive for those interested in joining. Other groups use meetups to have more formal gatherings or meetings, so this can be a great source of information to find like-minded people in your local area.

Other ways of growing your general network might involve joining professional organizations, like the Rotary Club or Bankers Association. For a more curated audience, consider local chapters of industry groups such as ISACA, ISSA, ISC2, OWASP, and InfraGard. Most of these organizations require a membership fee. Depending on your employment or financial situation, you'll have to decide if joining a chapter or two is worth the investment. Make sure you do your research first. Ask your online connections which ones they recommend. You might also want to consider going to local charity events or company-sponsored industry-specific presentations as ways to meet like-minded individuals. Other ways to build your network can include volunteering with local charities, schools, churches, or organizations, as this will also provide the opportunity to meet other professionals doing the same. You can also use these as opportunities to give back to the community by using the skills you are working on to help out these organizations. These meetups can be a win-win for all.

Using your general networking activities during your job search

Once you have found the events, meetings, or meetups of your choice, the in-person networking process is like online networking. You want to introduce yourself to the group members in a genuine manner, get to know them, and let them know you. Some groups recognize that they are a vehicle for job hunting and regularly make time during chapter meetings to introduce new members, guests, job hunters, and hiring managers. Be prepared with your 30-second bio (often referred to as your "elevator pitch"). Outside of the orchestrated introductions, come equipped with an exciting topic to discuss. This topic could be something recently in the news or even a story about yourself. But try not to make the conversation all about you; listen more than you talk. Remember that people like to talk about themselves. When the topic turns to you, be prepared to summarize your career and be willing to share your passions. Based on my experience, I recommend you not lead off by sharing that you are unemployed or looking for work. You should share your value and expertise first and then mention it later if an opportunity presents itself. These conversations provide you with a chance to position yourself as a contributing member of the community before asking for help.

Additionally, while unfair, people want to hire people who are employed. Being unemployed often begs why and people feel more confident about tempting you with an opportunity than rescuing you. One way to get past this is to mention that you are using the time between full-time situations to consult on projects that have always sparked your interest. Be prepared to back that up with details.

Don't be the one just collecting business cards or contact information for those that you met without really getting to know them. Three meaningful conversations are more valuable than 20 business cards for people you can't remember, as they are not likely to remember you, either. On that note, bring printed business cards with you, and use both sides of the card. Pictures are more memorable than words; put your photo on your card and use the back to highlight your top skills. These cards allow you to share something tangible with your new connections at the end of the encounter.

How to Build a Network that Works for You ~ Renee

"Weaponize Social Media for your career."[18]

A few times per week, Chris Foulon and I host a podcast and LinkedIn Live show, *Breaking into Cybersecurity*. We started this show to share insights directly from individuals who have broken into the industry in the past five years. Many of our guests have less than one year in the industry, and we are thrilled to have them participate! Before starting the podcast, we received numerous requests for coaching and mentorship for breaking into the field. Although well-intentioned, we realized that there was so much misinformation around breaking into the industry. Before coming to us, many of these people had asked seasoned cybersecurity professionals how to get into the field. The typical advice was to get a help desk job or become a system administrator. The pros went on to recommend spending 5-10 years growing in these roles before transitioning into security. I understand why their mentor gave this advice. Often, it was the advisor's own path and the paths of their peers. I agree that this is a path for some folks, but certainly not for all.

When we speak to people who are new to the industry, it's refreshing to hear their stories. We hear directly how they got their first job in the industry and pick up many gems for how others can break into cybersecurity. I was especially excited when hearing Chelin Sampson's story. Chelin is from South Africa and had recently taken a certification course. He was studying for the CISCO Certified CyberOps Associate exam and searching for a study group. When he couldn't find one, he created his own. Fast forward eighteen months, and he has over fifteen thousand members in the CISCO Cyber Ops

---

[18] Chelin Sampson https://www.linkedin.com/in/chelinsampson

Study Group on Facebook. He is now a frequent speaker at security conferences and has built his own network of cyber professionals.

I tell this story because he fulfilled a need for himself by creating his own community and network when he couldn't find one that met his needs. When he participated in our podcast, he gave one piece of very sage advice to "weaponize social media for your career." I immediately told him that I would "steal that saying" because it truly encompassed how someone with zero experience could create their own network in a matter of months on social media. It's fascinating to watch, and it's a piece of advice that I've often quoted since he came on the show.

The cyber community is like none other I have seen over my almost 20 years of recruiting in the technology space. I don't know of other conferences in IT that rival DefCon, BlackHat, BSides, and others. There is this fantastic network of overly willing people who help in whatever way they can and encourage others to get into the field. Another one of our podcast guests, Cornelius George, who came from the finance industry, shared a story. He said that he could never imagine reaching out to the CEO of JP Morgan Chase and getting a response. However, he talked about the numerous cyber executives who were willing to lend a helping hand as he started in the industry.

I have thought about the intimacy of this community over the years, and I believe it's due in part to the industry being so young that we must lean on each other heavily. The level of maturity in security programs varies, and jobs aren't fully standardized yet. There is also have the nature of the work and the desire to share best practices so that if criminals target one industry, we can quickly share information with our peers. Being a part of this network is how one gets early access to information and especially jobs. If you have heard of the hidden job market, this is one of them. Many positions don't hit the market. They are filled before they are even posted.

There are a few ways that I have seen others become heavily involved in the community and build robust networks. The three that will be discussed here are:

1. Volunteering for professional organizations
2. Participating and speaking at conferences
3. Starting your own community

Volunteering for professional organizations

One of the most straightforward ways to become a part of the community is by joining and volunteering in professional organizations. There is a plethora of organizations dedicated to various aspects of security. They provide resources, training, certifications, and a network of like-minded security professionals. Most organizations are eager to have volunteers with all types of skills to be a part of their committees and board. Even for a student or recent graduate, there are opportunities to join and get involved immediately. One of our podcast guests Maddy Pet, founded her Fortune 100 company's Women in Technology (WIT) chapter, and she has under five years in the industry.

By volunteering in professional organizations, you can showcase various skills that may not come through on your résumé. You can also network with seasoned professionals in the field who can guide you when you have questions about the various paths to take as you grow in your career. These same professionals have access to even more extensive networks, and they and their peers have access to jobs that may be unknown to you. For example, another podcast guest Gaylynn Fassler found out about her first job opportunity through volunteering for her local ISSA Triangle InfoSeCon, hosted by ISSA Raleigh Chapter. She recently gave her first talk with her manager at this same event. Now we'll segue into the next way to grow your network – participating and speaking at conferences.

Participating and speaking at conferences

Many cybersecurity conferences are huge events with thousands of attendees, and there is a myriad of talks and training opportunities. Then there are smaller, local events, with hundreds of attendees and a chance for you to jump in and help. As always, it's hard to find an organization that turns down volunteers. If you're willing to offer your time, it could be an opportunity to attend the event for free. You will immediately meet other professionals at all levels dedicated to enhancing the field.

You may think that there is no way you'd get a speaking engagement as a newbie, but that is not the case. Just like Gaylenn Fassler, many others have done the same. Would you be willing to provide interesting topics from a new person's perspective or partner with a more seasoned professional to co-deliver a talk? In addition, speaking at conferences will give you a significant boost to your network as people will want to connect and stay in touch with you as you explore more topics in the field.

Starting your own community or a chapter of an established one

Just like Chelin Sampson started his community, other people have started communities when they could not find what they needed. Lisa Jiggetts, the founder of the Women's Society of Cyberjutsu (WSC), started WSC to give women a place to learn and support each other. They now have multiple chapters all over the country. Mike Dahn and the other BSides founders wanted a conference dedicated to practitioners in more intimate settings. Their concept took off and is now a huge hit with the community.

If you see an opportunity to fill a void in security, consider connecting with a group of other people seeking the same thing and start your own!

Resources

Professional Organizations

- Cybercrime Magazine provides a list of 90 Cybersecurity Associations & Organizations.
- https://cybersecurityventures.com/cybersecurity-associations/

Conferences

- The InfoSec Conferences website provides an overview of most cybersecurity conferences. https://infosec-conferences.com/
- CSO Online also provides a list of top security conferences. https://www.csoonline.com/article/3155500/the-cso-guide-to-top-security-conferences.html

Chapter 5 – Key Points and Recommended Actions

The following is a quick summary of the key points from this chapter:

- There are many local, regional, and national organizations that you can join to meet people that share your passion for cybersecurity. The best approach is to mix online and in-person communities.
- Remember that networking is a two-way street. Be generous with your time and help where you can. Ideally, you'll be helping others before asking for the help that you need.
- The greatest value of networking when job hunting is to allow you to bypass posted jobs and tap the hidden openings filled without ever being publicized.
- A good network is helpful well beyond the transactional nature of job hunting and hiring. Establishing long-term relationships with people who can mentor you and mentoring those who aren't as far along in their cybersecurity journey as you transform an ordinary network into an extraordinary network.
- As has been true for decades, volunteering opens doors that would otherwise stay closed. Volunteer with our local professional groups, volunteer at your local school, but volunteer. Volunteering creates situations where you can establish relationships for mutual benefit while you and the other parties can have complete trust in each other's motives.

Chapter 6

Social Media

Introduction

Social media plays a crucial role in connecting people from all over the world. Consumers use it to develop and nurture relationships, share updates, stay connected and stay informed. Corporations also use it as a significant resource to access influencers, customers, partners, journalists, and potential recruits. In addition, social media provides organizations with a way to gather intelligence about how their products are used and perceived, what competitors are doing with their products, and provide a channel for direct customer feedback. However, when it comes to advancing their careers, people often do not consider that social media can be incredibly helpful.

Social media has become so pervasive that it is now a digital representation of you to a potential employer. Just as companies use social media for business purposes, they also use it to collect information about candidates they are interviewing for their open positions. This collection of social media intelligence has become the norm, which is why we wrote this chapter. But, first, you must be aware of the digital image you present to employers.

You will use social media throughout your career. Initially, focus on building a profile that informs hiring managers about your career goals, skills, and work experience. Then, as you become more comfortable with social promotion, you'll transition to publicly establishing your expertise. Eventually, you'll employ techniques that set you apart from the crowd and allow you to develop a persistent presence in the job market.

In the essays that follow, we'll teach you to document the accounts you have and ask yourself some in-depth questions about how you are portraying yourself both personally and professionally. Then once you have reflected, adjust your footprint where needed and start using social media as a digital business card to present who you are professionally and why you are the ideal candidate the employer should hire.

Approach this chapter with an open mind, have fun, and good luck!

Mature Your Social Media Footprint ~ Gary

In this chapter, I want to discuss why your social media footprint is essential. I am sure many of you are wondering why we are talking about social media. Why is your digital impression in social media relevant, and what does it have to do with building a career? Ten years ago, when social media was in its infancy, you would be correct to wonder; there would have been very little need to be concerned about how the professional world viewed your social media persona. However, in today's hyper-converged global business environment, you can expect three out of four hiring managers[19] will search for the candidate they are about to interview and review any social media profiles they find. Remember, the cybersecurity field is highly competitive, and those profiles tell a story about you; let's make sure it's a story you control.

To get started, I suggest you do an internet search on yourself and inventory your social media accounts, including the inactive ones. Once you have this list, I would recommend closing the inactive accounts first. Then I would review your remaining social media accounts and look for pictures, profanity-laden posts, or long rambling rants on subjects that could be divisive and consider removing them or at least cleaning them up. Next, how open are your active social accounts? I have known some people to have their accounts wide open to the world. I recommend keeping some things open to the public so potential employers can learn about you and saving the rest as private, only available to friends and family. Understand, I am not saying you need to be fake; I just want you to be smart. Remember, this is the beginning of building a personal brand that will follow you, and you will use it for your professional career.

---

[19] https://www.themuse.com/advice/job-seekers-social-media-is-even-more-important-than-you-thought

Now for our next step, a couple of points to assist you in building this brand. First, your profile image says a lot about you, so I would recommend putting the time and effort into getting several professional pictures taken and then periodically changing your profile image when you feel the need. Another point is to think of your social media accounts as potential assets to enhance your professional growth. I write, comment, and mentor many of my followers on LinkedIn. Anything I publish on LinkedIn, I also share on my Facebook, Medium, Twitter, and Reddit accounts. Use your accounts to drive your message if you have one or to develop one and have fun meeting new people as you grow your network. One final point is don't forget to put the link to your LinkedIn profile on your business card and your résumé.

Now let's look at several social media platforms and review some basic principles for using them.

- Facebook – Employers look at your Facebook account to see who you are outside of work. You don't need to hide your complete profile; review the pictures and content you have open to the public. Also, make sure to update your employment and educational information and have it public as well. If you are applying to companies with Facebook pages, it might be a good idea to "like" their page to show you are interested in them. If you like to write and have a blog, podcast, or share content, I highly recommend you add these to your professional status updates and make them public as well.

- LinkedIn – Before taking networking actions on LinkedIn, I would recommend that you first complete your profile. You want to keep your profile professional and add your professional picture and biography as an introduction. A good hack to get started is to search for people you know in the industry and review their profiles to get a feel for how you want to set up your profile. Next, look at joining groups to get started in discussions and only connect with people you know. This approach will provide you a basic professional profile to start, and then as you grow your network, add content such as articles so you can meet new people and get involved in the community.

- Twitter – Twitter is a social media platform where you can demonstrate your knowledge on a subject, share other people's information, and join ongoing discussions. If you have a Twitter account, I recommend using it and being active with the content you share. LinkedIn is more of a professional platform for business. Twitter can be the platform where you let your personality, experience, and thought leadership on subjects shine through. If you are using Twitter, follow experts and companies in your community of choice. Don't forget to create a biography using hashtag keywords. Be aware that recruiters will conduct searches using these keywords, so think carefully about which ones you use. Don't forget, just like LinkedIn or Facebook, your Twitter profile represents you to a hiring manager.

- GitHub – If you apply for software development positions, I recommend that you have an active account on GitHub or one of the other code repository sites. You want to demonstrate that you are involved in projects or show how the community uses your current projects. Also, if your résumé focuses on software development, don't forget to include your GitHub profile link.

- YouTube – YouTube is an excellent platform for any video content you create. I have known many thought leaders in cybersecurity who would do a video or podcast instead of writing an article. Either way, what is essential is that this is another way to grow your brand and interact with the cybersecurity community. Remember, if you use it, keep it current and be sure to share it across all of your social media accounts.

I know there are many more social media platforms available today, and in this chapter, I have only touched on several of the larger ones. The essential points I provided are to help you think about what your social media accounts say about you and how you use them effectively. I suggest you think about how social media has not only significantly impacted how we learn and play; it is now ingrained in how we work, how we grow our careers, and how we find jobs.

Social Media ~ Chris

It's essential to think of social media like other professional tools. While it can sometimes seem suited for personal time and connecting to people, using social media is about your intent when you use it. Having a social media presence can improve your chances of getting a new job or possibly damage your job prospects, depending on your social media use. The likelihood is that most individuals entering cybersecurity will already be using social media for personal and professional reasons.

There is a commonly known phrase saying that "if something gets posted on the internet, it is there forever." While this statement might seem dramatic, some services scan, catalog, and index much of the internet. Knowing this fact will allow you to decide what, how, and when to post things online. In addition, understanding the features, settings, and use cases for the different social media platforms will allow you to control what information gets published and who might have access to it.

This chapter will focus on a couple of different social media sites and the best ways to use them to help you break into the cybersecurity industry. My primary focus will be on LinkedIn and Twitter, and I'll cover some of the other sites or social portals you can use to learn more about and connect with the community.

LinkedIn has become the primary platform for recruiting, job hunting, and professional networking. For many people, a LinkedIn profile might be their first impression of you for many people, so you want to present yourself in the best possible light. Later in this chapter, we will discuss tips on polishing your profile. In addition to connecting people, LinkedIn provides a platform for sharing news, articles, forming public and private groups, and having discussions via posts, and gives users the ability to interact with connections using direct messages.

Outside of LinkedIn and news sites such as Ars Technica, CSO Online, Dark Reading, Wired, and Twitter, Reddit is a popular platform for the information security community for sharing information and discussing topics in public. We will discuss ways to capitalize on this later in this chapter. We will also briefly discuss other valuable tools, including StackOverflow, YouTube, Twitch, Discord, and Slack. So let us move forward and learn how to use social media to your advantage as you transition into the industry.

Think before you post

As mentioned earlier, it is crucial to think before you post as screenshots or copies of your posts can be taken out of context. A helpful mindset for you to consider is if you were to have this conversation with your grandmother, or with friends in your church, or with your children, what they would think about you if they saw this post? Keep in mind that your LinkedIn profile and your social media presence are freely available. People who want to know about you, including potential employers, will likely be researching your online profile. What is publicly known about you will form the basis of their first impression, and their hiring decision. Looking at a social media presence is the most common way to vet people in the digital age today.

When engaging online about emotional or controversial topics, people sometimes do not think about their statements' impact. The disconnect in understanding your words' impact might be because of perceived anonymity or not getting the value of body language feedback when engaging online. The lack of a filter in these situations is what comes back to damage your online reputation. Statements on LinkedIn, Twitter, or other very public platforms can affect your employment. As these examples from *Workopolis*[20] and *The Muse*[21] show, people have been fired over their social media posts. Hopefully, you can learn from the mistakes of others and become more mindful of what you post online.

The internet never forgets (but you can try to clean it up)

Here are some of the helpful tips I have for cleaning up and improving your social profiles and images:

1. Google yourself and see what comes up; you may be surprised with the results. I would look at all the findings, even those several pages deep, to see if they are related to you. Do not forget to look at Google images.

2. Look through your existing social media accounts for unflattering, controversial, and offensive posts or pictures. I recommend that you take a very conservative approach to what you deem acceptable. If you don't want to part with some favorite memories, remove them online and save them on your machine, or mark them as private and only viewable by family. Do not forget about pictures where you are tagged. Consider asking the person who posted the picture to remove the tag or the photo if possible. Some social media sites allow you to remove yourself from tags on images of others. Do not forget to clean up the profile sections of those pages, where you describe your interests, likes, dislikes, or joined various groups on that social platform.

3. Delete, deactivate, or make old accounts private. You might have forgotten about that old Myspace or GeoCities page you

---

[20] https://careers.workopolis.com/advice/6-people-who-were-fired-for-social-media-posts/
[21] https://www.themuse.com/advice/yes-you-can-get-fired-for-your-social-media-posts-9-times-people-learned-this-lesson-the-hard-way

created in high school, but the internet did not. Try looking for them using your old aliases and email addresses.

Other useful tips and resources:

- Affordable Colleges Online has helpful information for students to clean up their online presence[22]
- McAfee has a couple of valuable resources for cleaning up and curating your online persona[23] [24]
- The Muse[25], Lifehacker[26], and Free Code Camp[27] all weigh in with great articles as well

Treat your social media profiles like real estate; let them work for you.

Now that you have cleaned up your social media profiles and removed anything that might embarrass you or hurt your chances of getting a job, it is time to turn those profiles into digital assets that will help you grow into your new career. Since social media profiles and websites will be the first impression many recruiters, hiring managers, and colleagues have of you, you want to make them shine.

LinkedIn

This social media platform started as a professional networking site for individuals to get to know each other professionally, share and

---

[22] https://www.affordablecollegesonline.org/college-resource-center/college-students-clean-up-your-online-profiles-now/
[23] https://www.mcafee.com/blogs/consumer/family-safety/10-easy-ways-to-clean-up-curate-your-social-media/
[24] https://www.mcafee.com/blogs/consumer/family-safety/10-easy-ways-to-clean-up-curate-your-social-media/
[25] https://www.themuse.com/advice/8-easy-ways-clean-up-social-media-job-search
[26] https://lifehacker.com/how-to-delete-your-old-tweets-and-favs-before-your-enem-1821062277
[27] https://www.freecodecamp.org/news/how-to-build-an-amazing-linkedin-profile-15-proven-tips/amp/

find new jobs, or engage in discussions with other professionals. It has grown to include an integrated training platform, a recruiting platform for those looking to hire, a sales platform for those looking for prospects, and more. The core aspect of LinkedIn is the profile page for an individual or company that shares the information about who they are.

Here are some tips to help with creating a great profile:

Start with having a professional headshot. It is usually the first thing someone sees when searching. If a professional headshot is out of your reach, you can use the portrait mode on your smartphone to take a great headshot, even one with the nice-looking background blur.

Ensure that your profile is up to date. I know this should go without saying, but I often see profiles that have not been updated in years. Even when you are not job hunting, you should be continuously updating your profiles with new content.

1. Headline – This is a statement about you, usually under your profile image, and is the second thing someone notices. This headline should be a one or two-sentence message that engages readers and makes them want to find out more about you or what makes you unique.

2. About/Summary – As the name implies, this section allows you to provide readers will a high-level overview of who you are, what you have accomplished, your goals, and what sets you apart from others in the field.

3. Experience – This section is a virtual version of your résumé. The key here is not to make it a replica of your résumé. You can give a lot more content, and you should use it to supplement your résumé. Show results, accomplishments,

and other reasons why someone would want to connect with you or hire you.

4. Other sections include areas for education, certifications, skills, and recommendations from others.

Post, engage, and interact with relevant content and groups. This engagement will likely get you visibility with possible hiring managers, recruiters, and colleagues. Additionally, this allows you to highlight your skills, competencies, and areas of expertise.

Having a blog, podcast, or website where you share this content is also helpful. These sites can be an area where you can continually add new content, bring value to the community, and separate yourself from other candidates.

Twitter

If you aren't very familiar with how Twitter is used, it is one of the most helpful social media platforms for a member of the information security community to get to know. It can provide you both with access to both influential people in the industry and information you might not otherwise find. Here is a short primer on Twitter.

There are some core concepts you need to understand to master your use of Twitter:

- Tweet – Compared to other social media platforms, Twitter started very much as a one-way conversation of you sharing a "tweet" or update to those who follow you. It has since grown to where you can reply, re-tweet, (meaning share the tweet with or without comments), and like a tweet. Each of these actions places content on your feed, which your followers then see.

- Followers – You do not need to know someone to follow them, and you can follow as many people as you like. In popular culture, you might follow movie stars, and in the case of information security, you might follow security researchers. This allows you to engage in these conversations by providing your own commentary. While it might be tempting to follow someone only for the fact that they followed you, I would not recommend this. This could clutter up your feed with more noise than signal.

- Feed – Your Twitter feed is where you land when you log on to Twitter and it shows the tweets and re-tweets of accounts you follow. Follow only the people and companies you want to hear from, so the information you want to consume is easier to find.

- Hashtags (#) – Mechanisms for highlighting keywords within a tweet both for effect and to group tweets into threads for easy searching. For example, #cybersecurity might be used to highlight cybersecurity conversations, and you can also then search for that #cybersecurity across the platform for all other tweets, which are again using this tag. When a # starts to appear in many tweets, it is trending at the time, as it allows it to be used for sentiment and pattern.

- Bookmarks – As the name implies, this feature allows you to bookmark tweets so that you can revisit them in the future. Bookmarks become helpful if you are researching a topic and would like to review them later.

- Lists – A way of categorizing people you follow into groups so that you can selectively try to filter what appears in your feed. You can notify or choose not to tell someone when you add them to a list of yours. I have noticed that I tend to get added to a list of security researchers or intelligence sources because of the articles I love to share.

- Public and private tweets – For the most part, you will see the tweets of most people; the few exceptions are those who make their tweets private and need to approve their followers and those who have blocked you for a particular reason.

Now that you have a basic understanding of Twitter, you can use it to keep up with what is happening in the information security community. You will find that security researchers will publish their finds to Twitter with links to their research, so it helps you keep a pulse on what is happening. It can also be a drama-filled community with strong opinions on all sides, so it is up to you to choose what you would like to gather from your experience.

Wired Magazine has published a helpful article[28] on Twitter and making the best use of it.

Other helpful social media sites/platforms which I will go into fewer details include:

- **YouTube** – allows you to look up videos for learning new skills for free from both industry professionals and those just looking to share their passions. Be aware that YouTube can become a rabbit hole where you lose all sense of time and spend hours and hours, so I recommend finding targeted videos or topics you would like to view and sticking to them. You can also record the content of your own and share it with others, which might be an excellent way to stand out from other candidates on the job market.

- **Slack** (https://slack.com/) – while this platform started as an enterprise collaboration and messaging platform, its free edition has risen in popularity for creating similar online communities for companies, groups, or those with similar

---

[28] https://www.wired.com/story/how-to-setup-twitter-search-hashtag-and-login-help/

ideas to interact. It allows for different channels based on conversations at a group level and direct messaging options to members. Slack recently added voice and video chat capabilities within the free platform. The Enterprise version has a lot more integrations and features.

- **Discord** (https://discord.com/) – started as a platform in which gamers can verbally interact with each other while playing games but has evolved to include a message forum and voice channels. You will notice that many of the well-respected security research companies are developing communities on this platform to stay connected to the community in a more personal way than Twitter or their website. Discord allows users to create sections for different topics and foster different types of conversions within their channel. Discord has voice, text, and direct messaging options.

- **Twitch** (https://www.twitch.tv/) – like YouTube, is a video streaming platform but started as a way to live stream videos to viewers. Like Discord, it began with a focus on the gaming market. This platform is useful for learning from someone sharing how-to videos.

Maximize the potential of your social media profiles

Now that you know how the major social media platforms work and how to create a profile, it is time to go out and build yours to be a shining representation of who you are. Besides helping you continuously learn new information. They provide you with a great way to stand apart in the information community by sharing the information you learned or researched with others in the community. Sharing could be in videos (YouTube, Twitch), written form (blogs and articles on LinkedIn), and engaging with the community on the different social media platforms.

Remember to be humble; there will always be others who know more than you about a topic or approach things differently. Be open to continuous learning and sharing. Diverse opinions, views, and backgrounds all help us become a more resilient community. Be who you are; you do not have to become part of the crowd. Just be smart with the image you put out there, and it will pay dividends for you.

Social Media ~ Renee

A few months ago, my recruiter colleagues and I hosted a podcast focused on what we look for when searching on social media for candidates. We are usually searching for specific skillsets shown through keywords; however, a few things came out of that discussion that I think were pretty surprising to some of the attendees.

Surprising insights

The first thing that seemed to be a surprise to many, is that recruiters have tools that can look across various social media platforms. Many of us can research and gain visibility into a person's entire social media footprint. As Gary and Chris have written, you will want to be careful about what you put on social media on the different platforms. You may think that recruiters and managers do not have access to specific platforms. However, we can and will find out what you're doing and saying online. The point is not to suggest you stay silent about topics about which you are passionate. I'm telling you that you should know that it is difficult to remain anonymous and that anything you post online can and will likely be found. If you are searching for a position, you will want to consider how a hiring authority might view your comments. There have been many recent incidents of offers being rescinded based on comments made online. I can imagine that many of the people posting the comments thought the posts were harmless internet chatter. Unfortunately, the words cost them their jobs.[29]

---

[29] For examples, see: https://generalcounselnews.com/fpa-androvett-bad-judgment-on-social-media-may-lead-to-job-offer-withdrawals/ and https://www.insider.com/college-student-deloitte-internship-anti-all-lives-matter-tiktok-2020-7

Skill sets required for the job

First, let me share what happens when a recruiter receives a request to look for a person to fill a job opening. The hiring manager reaches out to their recruiting partner with the specific criteria they're looking for in the person they would like to hire. Let's take an identity and access management (IAM) analyst role as an example. The leader will often look for someone who already has some IAM experience, even if it's limited. Depending on the role's level, it could be gained from an internship, self-directed project, or volunteer experience.

As a recruiter, one of the first places I will go to look for profiles is on LinkedIn. My initial search will be to find people who have "IAM" or "identity and access management" in their social media profiles. If the manager has a specific tech stack, it's ideal to have experience in those technologies. So, if this client uses CyberArk, my next step could be to search "CyberArk." I will also search CyberArk's competitors for IAM and use the competitors in my search as well. After I've exhausted LinkedIn, I may go on Twitter to see if people are commenting about IAM or CyberArk. I will assume that these people making comments are likely in the field and working in IAM. I will take this information and cross-reference it against other social media accounts to see if these people look like they could be a good match. This research continues on different social media sites until I've found enough people to reach out to for this role.

This example is why we recruiters stress that you should have as much detail in your LinkedIn profile as possible. If you have IAM experience, but your profiles don't say you have it, we will take the path of least resistance and look for people who have the words spelled out in their profile. If the profile has the experience shown multiple times, that's a bigger incentive to reach out to that person. These are the people who get bombarded with recruitment requests because their profile "screams" their experience and has the keywords that managers seek.

It also helps the hiring managers. I have seen instances where a manager declines to move forward with a person's consideration because they can't decipher if they have the experience based on the profile. You don't want to be passed over before the process even begins due to a slim LinkedIn profile.

Again, even if you are transitioning with zero "real-world experience," please showcase any experience that you do have. This can be as simple as highlighting the projects you completed in your college coursework or your home lab. It could be volunteer work or internships. I have filled jobs where the hiring manager asked for "anyone with a little bit of experience including an internship."

Always put yourself in the shoes of the manager when developing your online presence. Would a manager be able to find me? Would they know that I have these skills? Would the comments that I make seem offensive or combative? Is this the image I want to portray to the leaders of the company?

Pick something you are passionate about and discuss it

One of the fastest ways to get noticed on social media is by discussing a topic you're passionate about. When I started in security, my leader had all the newbies review the CISSP domains. He wasn't concerned with us taking the test, but he made us pick two areas that interested us and asked us to do further research in those areas. This was such a helpful exercise. Very quickly, I learned cryptography was not for me. I also realized which areas were more interesting to me. You might consider doing the same. If something interests you, you are more likely to do more research, dig deeper into the topic and be curious about the subject. You are also more likely to have something to say about it on social media. This will also keep you focused, so you won't feel that you have to comment on everyone's posts.

Consider posting your own content and engaging with other people about their content. Quite often, engaging with others will get you noticed faster, especially if they are popular and are a leader in the field. The rule of thumb is to make ten comments on others' posts for every post you create. If you do that three times per week, you will be well on your way to gaining leaders' attention.

One way to engage in others' content is to make a thoughtful response to what someone has posted and add your thought-provoking questions.

Creating video

Although YouTube has been around for over 15 years, LinkedIn just recently started allowing video in 2017. It's one of the few social media platforms that are new to video, and the exposure is enormous. You can also apply for access to Livestream. As of the writing of this book, that option is still in beta.

My podcast co-hosts and I have been challenging job hunters to create a video of themselves. We have encouraged our viewers to make a 30-60 second elevator pitch speaking to who they are and why they are great candidates. The first person who took us up on the challenge received an internship offer in less than 24 hours! Within the next 30 days, she had a full-time offer. Video cuts through the noise, and this is especially helpful on LinkedIn. And it works!

Take your camera phone out and record why you would be an asset to someone's organization. Talk about your passions and your strengths. Practice it a few times, so it's natural, and you get the nervousness out. When you're done, post it on LinkedIn and see how quickly you can get interviews. Recruiters, especially managers looking for talent, will be quick to reach out since they can see your enthusiasm shine through.

In summary, recruiters and hiring managers are on social media just like everyone else. Ensure that you have a presence that shows a hiring manager your passions and insight as you look for opportunities.

Chapter 6 – Key Points and Recommended Actions

The following is a quick summary of the key points from this chapter:

- Your presence on social media, from your LinkedIn profile to your Twitter handle, and all points in between, are essential tools for your job search and career management.
- Start by cleaning up your public presence. While it is true that notorious posts are hard to erase, the unfortunate content on the average profile consists of off-color comments and inappropriate pictures. These should be removed and privacy settings inspected to ensure that your visibility is appropriate for your circumstances.
- Weaponize your social media presence. Your social media strategy is not merely defensive or static. After you have updated your content to put your best foot forward, you can step your game up to connection, engagement, and contribution. Use social media to build relationships and engage with your community.
- Social media is probably the greatest source of free intel in the world. Learn how to search for information on companies you are targeting for employment and key players at those companies and use the information to gauge your relative suitability for positions compared to your peers.
- Companies regularly post about themselves, and so do their competitors. Product launches and public mishaps are regularly discussed, and you should always be on top of what is happening in your field and to your targets.
- For people willing to put themselves forward, take social media posts to the next level and shoot videos. Pictures are worth a thousand words, and moving pictures are worth millions.

Section 4

The Job Search

Introduction

To "hunt something up" means to "search until found." And while Gary, Chris, and Renee have made the point throughout this book that you're on more of a journey than a hunt, the fact is that at times you will need to take another job. We haven't lost sight of the main point of this book, which is developing your cybersecurity career and, yes, breaking into cybersecurity.

Another fascinating word we collectively use when talking about the process of hiring and job hunting is "vetting." Recruiters and hiring managers vet candidates. We vet prospective employers, and we vet potential jobs. To "vet" was originally a horse-racing term, meaning that a horse had to be checked by a veterinarian for health and soundness before being allowed to race. That's an excellent way to think of the process of vetting the jobs we are considering. We want to check them for health and soundness. What can we find out about the company's culture, technologies, and our prospective role? Will this job help us advance our careers?

The following four chapters represent the largest section of the book. The first three, dealing with your résumé, the job search, and preparing for the interview, involve a lot of research. In a sense, you are vetting yourself, your potential job, and your potential manager and colleagues. The last chapter in this section helps you understand the recruiter's role. The recruiter is often the first person who will vet you, so understanding how to work with the recruiter is crucial to your job search. Enjoy the hunt!

Chapter 7

Building Your Cyber Résumé

Introduction

"Most illustrious Lord" is how Leonardo da Vinci began what is widely believed to be the first résumé.[30] We're not inclined to give quite so much deference to our employers anymore. He went on to refer to other artisans who might be competing for the same position as having produced somewhat commonplace outcomes. We don't tend to disparage or even reference other candidates when writing a résumé or interviewing for a job. After these two elements, which are thankfully no longer in vogue, he moved on to what could be considered one of the most effective ways to target a résumé. He listed eleven specific things he could do that were directly relevant to the position he sought. In the following three essays, Gary, Chris, and Renee will provide their thoughts on résumé writing. You'll notice, as Renee makes clear, that the more things have changed, the more they remain the same.

Gary goes deep into how he has set up his résumé by including marked-up snippets from one of the résumés he used for job hunting. Then, by breaking the résumé into five parts and discussing what he's trying to accomplish in each piece, he gives you valuable insights that will help you with your résumé.

Chris breaks down the different types of résumés and how people in various stages of the transition to a career in cybersecurity might use them. His descriptions of company- or position-specific and role-

---

[30] The Italian Renaissance Reader, Julia Conaway Bondanella, Plume; Illustrated edition (November 13, 1987)

specific résumés and how to use each effectively provide you with valuable knowledge for targeting your use of these critical tools.

Renee lends the value of her more than twenty years as a recruiter to review the sections of the résumé and tell you what she would look for in the résumés of candidates she considers for the positions she fills.

How should you approach reading this chapter? Why not print out a copy of your résumé, grab a red pen, and get to work? The best résumé won't get you a job, but it might just get you the interview.

So how did Leonardo and Gary do with their résumés? They both got the job.

Writing a Cybersecurity Résumé ~ Gary

In 2007 when I was retiring from the military, I felt lost and anxious about my family and what would happen to us. It is stressful for most veterans as we "transition" and step away from a life of service into the private sector. For me, I had spent the previous two decades of my life serving my country and in effect protecting private industry, but I had no idea how to work in it. As my time on active duty came to a close, I attended the one-week transition class that was supposed to tell me everything I needed to know about becoming a civilian. I can't explain how every night I came home to my wife and two young children during that week and was terrified. I felt I had skillsets and experience that should get my family and me a well-paying job, but one of the most challenging tasks to learn was communicating my value in a résumé.

Fast forward to today, and I find that many of the people I mentor, both veterans and civilians, who want a career in the cyber community, still find the résumé to be one of the most challenging tools for them to master. I say "tool" because that is what it is, a strategic communication tool we use to tell the value story we bring to a potential employer and land an interview. Keeping this in mind, my contribution to this chapter will be a how-to guide for developing your first cyber résumé. In preparing for this chapter, I reviewed many old copies of previous résumés and résumés peers have shared with me over the years to make sure I provide you with a tool that is current for today's business needs.

This chapter is for you in the spirit of giving back to a new generation of cyber professionals joining our community. Don't view it as a set-in-stone guide but as a suggestion on how you might collect your thoughts and put them to paper.

I'm going to begin with the basics. I look at my résumé as having five core parts with an optional component for those who wish to list their technical expertise.

Part 1 – Résumé Title and Intro

I use the résumé title and introduction part of my résumé to list my name and contact information and describe who I am as a professional. In this section I also include a listing of expertise/skill sets (technical/soft) to quickly note the value I bring to an organization.

Figure 7.1 Resume 1 of 6

Part 2 – Professional Experience

In the next section, professional experience, you list the most current position and work yourself backward. I have been in the workforce for twenty-plus years. With that said, I don't list two decades' worth of employers. I've written this version of my résumé for technology and security executive positions, so I have decided to cover only the last fifteen years of experience. I feel this period is enough to demonstrate I have the knowledge, skill sets, and leadership experience for any position that I am applying for, but keep in mind this is unique to each person. I once knew a long-time security executive who felt he needed to list everything he ever did, and his résumé was eleven pages long. Astonishingly, he had a hard time understanding why people didn't want to read it. Again, focus your résumé on the role – you are telling a value story of how you meet the requirements for a job, not your life story. One final point I want to make here, pay attention to the title you list for each previous position.

In my example, I note the company name, my position, number of employees, annual revenue, and time frame. I do this so a potential employer can understand the breadth of the responsibilities I held in each position. There is a difference between being a CISO for a company with fifty employees and five million dollars in revenue and a CISO for a company with ten thousand employees and four billion dollars in revenue. This distinction doesn't belittle the effort of a CISO for a smaller business, it just acknowledges that there are differences in scale, responsibility, and accountability, and you want that captured in your résumé. After the job title, I write an introductory paragraph to explain the position and why the company hired me. Again, this is a personal preference. I have seen basic introductions that were stock job descriptions, and I have seen problem statements written to describe specifically what the applicant was hired to fix – it's up to you.

As a hiring manager, when looking at candidates' résumés, whether their experience comes from an SMB or from a large company, I look for the breadth of their responsibility and the depth of experience. What I mean by that is, did they work on multiple projects? Did they lead some of those projects? What impact did those projects have on the business? Are they involved in the cyber community? Are they actively working on projects with a layer of complexity? What I am looking for is a continuous drive for professional development and someone who brings with them a passion for the field. Yes, I like people who are just as motivated as I am about security because they get things done and are fun to work with.

> Servant Leadership, Coaching and Mentoring   Disaster Recovery & Business Continuity Planning
> Incident Response & Management   CIS 20, NIST CSF, ISO 27001, PCI, GDPR
>
> **EDUCATION AND SPECIALIZED TRAINING**
> - **MBA**, San Diego State University — San Diego, CA
> - **BS in Information Systems Management,** University of Maryland University College - College Park, MD
> - **Professional Development Certificate,** Advanced Computer Security - Stanford University, San Francisco CA
> - **Clearance** - Active "Secret" Security Clearance, DHS sponsoring Agency
>
> **PROFESSIONAL EXPERIENCE**
> *Webroot Software, San Diego CA*   *2017 to Present*
> *750+ Employees, Global Cybersecurity Company, $500+ Million Revenue*
> Vice President of Cyber, Risk & Compliance, Global Chief Information Security Officer — (CISO)
>
> Webroot is one of the largest privately held cybersecurity companies that is experiencing dynamic growth and due to this rapid expansion the company required a CISO with extensive experience building cybersecurity programs and evangelizing the value of cybersecurity to executive leadership, employees, customers and the community at large. In 2017, Webroot hired myself as its first Global CISO. My mandate, advise the board of directors and executive leadership on protecting critical proprietary data resources and oversee the development and implementation of all information security strategies, including Webroot's security standards, procedures and internal controls. As CISO, my mission includes creating a "risk aware" culture that emphasizes the high clue of securing and protecting customer information entrusted to Webroot and contributing to product strategy by guiding the efficacy of Webroot's security portfolio of services for its global customers.
>
> - As the CISO, I architected Webroot's first corporate cybersecurity and risk management department. I established the Cloud Security & Governance team, Cybersecurity Architecture & Risk Mtigation team and the Cybersecurity Operations team to provide risk management services to this organization of 20+ departments and product development teams. As part of architecting this enterprise wide security program based on NIST and ISO standards and created a three-year strategy to meet NIST certification requirements. and Compliance, I am the lead project creation of all required corporate infor

[Callout: I like to use LinkedIn in the footer]

[Callout: Introduction, how you came to position and your mandate or breadth of responsibility]

www.linkedin.com/in/ghayslip/

Figure 7.2 Resume 2 of 6

Part 3 – Employment Description

This part of the résumé is where you describe what you did in your previous positions. You should document specific work experience, initiatives, projects, and duties that you feel demonstrate you have the requirements for that new job, and they should give you that interview. I write this part of the résumé after the introductory paragraph. This part contains at least three bulleted statements about accomplishments that I achieved in that position. I try to make sure the statements do not use acronyms, and I try to use numbers to give the comments more context for the reader.

One last point before we move on – in the image below, you will note that I like to put my LinkedIn address in the footer. I have seen people put contact information here, the web address to their own website, or a link to the GitHub project list. I like to use LinkedIn because it provides more insight into my commitment to our security community. Again, it's a personal preference, and I would recommend that you at least put some contact information like an email address in the footer.

> Security Framework (CSF) as its core risk management standard. As the senior security visionary for the City, I oversaw the management of all security architecture, and the complete development and implementation of the enterprise security program that provided risk mitigation services to 25 networks and 40,000+ endpoints. In this position as CISO and Deputy CIO, I built collaborative partnerships with local, regional, state, and federal agencies suck as the Law Enforcement Coordination Center, Regional Terrorism Threat Assessment Center (RTTAC) Computer and Technology Crime High Technology High-Tech (CATCH) Response Team, California Off the federal Department of Homeland Security (DHS)
>
> - As CISO, I oversaw, evaluated and managed all corporate information security controls, risk assessments, and collaborated with departmental/BU's, end users) stakeholder's. This internal collaboration resulted in a reduction of governance "Segregation of Duties" errors by 30% enabling the City to meet its SOC 2 compliance requirements.
> - As the City's lead security executive, I architected and built an enterprise cyber security suite with minimal funding by securing federal grants and partnering with six local cybersecurity startups. These partnerships provided the City with cutting edge technologies and enabled the creation of a Security Operations Center (SOC) that directly resulted in the reduction of infected workstation assets from an average of 165 per month to 30 per month. This reduction directly equates to a savings of $1.6 Million annually in operations costs and a savings of 300 manhours per month of lost productivity.
> - As Deputy CIO, I developed the City's first enterprise Information Security Incident Response Program, defining security escalation response procedures and security incident response workflows. This program was instrumental in protecting the revenue assets of this $4 Billion organization in its contracted data-centers and hybrid cloud environments that averaged 500,000+ attacks per day against its infrastructure.

Annotation: After position introduction, have at least three bullets and ensure you use numbers use to demonstrate value include financial,

Figure 7.3 Resume 3 of 6

Part 4 – Community and Executive Affiliations

This part of the résumé follows professional experience. I have seen some people put education and certifications after professional experience because this section doesn't apply to them. There aren't any hard-set rules on what to list after the professional experience, so I leave that up to you. I use this section to note organizational boards that I work with because my résumé is focused on executive and leadership positions. This section is necessary for me to show that I am a security thought leader, and I am heavily involved in our community. For a new security analyst or a security architect, if you have volunteered for events like BSides or DefCon you might list it here, along with any local events you have participated in. Otherwise, use the "Memberships" header listed in Part 5 below to note professional groups you are a member of and any community involvement such as Boy Scouts or Cyber Patriots.

BOARDS AND AFFILIATIONS

National Technology Security Coalition
Member – Advisory Board

- The National Technology Security Coalition (NTSC) is a non preeminent advocacy voice for CISOs. Through dialogue, edu and private sector stakeholders around policies that improve n

[Callout: After Professional Experience, list any Boards or Affiliations (Professional Groups) – Make sure to annotate your position]

San Diego CISO Round Table
Member - Board of Directors   2015 - Present

- The San Diego CISO Round Table was founded in 2007. The Round Table consists of many different industries verticals to include Energy sector, Critical Infrastructure, Medical/Hospitals, Defense, Electronics, Banking/Financial, E-commerce, and others. The focus of this group is to share current threats, Intel, and concerns as well as mentor the younger/newer CISO's within the community through promoting an atmosphere of learning, information sharing, and engagement for all members.

InfraGard - San Diego Members Alliance
IT Sector Co-Chief, Member - Board of Directors   2015 - Present

- The National InfraGard Program began as a pilot project in 1996 when the Cleveland FBI Office asked local computer security professionals to assist the FBI in determining how to better protect critical information systems in the public

Figure 7.4 Resume 4 of 6

Part 5 – Education, Certifications, and Memberships

For most of us, this final section is where I would list education, certifications, memberships, and published works. I have seen the education and certifications part collapsed into one segment, which can be an option for you if you are entry-level and just beginning in the cybersecurity field. One note of caution, if you are listing online training courses that you have completed, please refrain from including a long list of professional courses. It is not very professional, and whoever is reading your résumé will tune out and throw it away. You might instead want to say something like, "Completed over 40 Udemy courses on topics such as encryption, business operations, network security, artificial intelligence...". That is an excellent way to note the training you have completed without turning your résumé into a novel.

EDUCATION AND SPECIALIZED TRAINING
- MBA, San Diego State University – San Diego, CA
- BS in Information Systems Management, University of Maryland
- Professional Development Certificate, Advanced Computer Security
- Clearance - Active "Secret" Security Clearance, DHS sponsoring Agency

PROFESSIONAL CERTIFICATIONS & TRAINING
- Certified Information Systems Security Professional (CISSP) - #98865
- Information Systems Security Engineering Professional (CISSP-ISSEP) - #98865
- Certified Information Systems Auditor (CISA) - #0971819
- Certified in Risk and Information Systems Control (CRISC) - #1001114
- ISO/IEC 27001 – Information Security Management – Provisional Auditor - #PECB-ISPA1000954-2018-05
- Linux Professional Institute (LPI) – LPIC-1 "Linux Administrator"- #LPI000276294
- Computer Technology Industry Association (CompTIA) **Linux+** - #COMP001001325131
- Certificate of Cloud Security Knowledge (CCSK) - #650184717736

MEMBERSHIPS AND SPEAKING ENGAGEMENTS
- Information Systems Audit and Control Association – (ISACA), San Diego Chapter - Member
- Information Systems Security Association – (ISSA), San Diego Chapter - Member
- Boy Scouts of America, Sweetwater Council – Merit Badge Counselor
- Autism Society of America – San Diego Chapter - Member
- Speaker – RSA, ISSA, ISACA, RIMS, Splunk Live, Gartner Security & Risk Management Summit, Gartner - Catalyst Conference, Municipal Information Systems Association of California (MISAC) and Blackhat (Vendor role).

PUBLISHED WORKS
- Book - *CISO Desk Reference Guide, A practical Guide for CISO's Volume 2* – April 2018 (Amazon)
- Book - *CISO Desk Reference Guide, A practical Guide for CISO's Volume 1* – 2016 (Amazon)
- Articles for ITSP Magazine, SC Magazine, Information Week, DarkReading, CSO Magazine, Wired, Security Current

> After Boards and Affiliations, list Education, Professional Certs/Training, Professional Group memberships or speaking engagements and any Published Works.

Figure 7.5 Resume 5 of 6

I hope this brief description of how to organize and put together your thoughts and information into a résumé has provided some value for you. Please note that nowhere in my résumé do I list my hobbies or any references. I have had peers, and mentors, reiterate time and again that your résumé should be a professional document, and you should strive to keep it that way. You can list your hobbies on other social media platforms, and you can provide a list of references when you get the job offer. If you are transitioning from military service, please take a look at the cybersecurity field. We need your talent, and it's a chance to continue serving.

One final note, I want to add an optional section that I believe would be important for analysts, engineers, and architects. In this section, I would list specific technical expertise. It is for those of us who are writing technical résumés versus management résumés.

Part 6 – Optional for Technical Résumés

*** OPTIONAL
TECHNOLOGIES, SERVICES, PROTOCOLS, TOOLS & PROGRAMMING LANGUAGES
- List of Security/Network Equipment Have Experience With
    - Firewalls, IDS/IPS, IAM, SIEM, EDR, Endpoint
- List of Services
    - SAAS, PAAS, IAAS, May also list some large SAAS platforms like ServiceNow or Sales Force
- Protocols
    - IP, DNS, ENCRYPTION, FTP, SSH, SIP
- Tools
    - KALI, COBALT, MALTEGO, METASPLOIT, SPLUNK, BRIGHTCLOUD
- Programming Languages
    - Python, JAVA, R, C++

***Optional – Have used this for when applying to technical positions where you list the various technologies, languages, services etc. you have experience in. This is not used once you move into Management positions unless they want to know your background.

Figure 7.6 Resume 6 of 6

Building and Tailoring Your Résumé for Success ~ Chris

The résumé is your ticket to make it past the HR screeners and Applicant Tracking Systems (ATS) and onto the desks of hiring managers. Depending on where you are in your career, you may or may not have all the experience needed for the role you are applying for, but don't let that slow you down; there are ways to get past the job history requirements and show that you have the essential attributes to perform well in the role. I will give you some tips below to help you.

There are several factors for you to consider when crafting your résumé. The first is to make sure your résumé is relevant to the position posted. This helps you get to the human screeners. You also need to line up the skills, certifications, education, and experience. Keeping this format is important to satisfy the automated screeners that are scoring your résumé. And finally, you want your résumé to stand out from the résumés of all the other candidates who have applied.

You can take a several approaches when designing your résumé; you can have a role-specific résumé, a position/company-specific résumé, or just a general, all-inclusive résumé. I do not recommend submitting the all-inclusive résumé because it tends to include too much information, some of which may not be relevant to the specific role and company. In addition, these résumés tend not to score high with an ATS, and if they do reach HR or hiring managers, they fail to hold the human's interest because busy people don't have the time to read through detailed and lengthy résumés. But this does not mean that the general résumé doesn't have its purpose. It can be a great way to collect and maintain a comprehensive summary of your experience, past roles and responsibilities, results you may emphasize, and projects you have worked on throughout your career. You can also include school courses, internships, and volunteer experience.

You never know when an internship might become a relevant experience for an interesting open job.

I typically recommend going with the role-specific résumé or the position/company-specific résumé. Still, these tailored résumés each have their purpose, so having both might be useful. Let's dive into their structure and use cases.

Position/Company-Specific Résumé

This résumé style is tailored to the company and the position you are applying for and requires the most time and effort to create. When you realize that you may apply for between 20 and 200 jobs, depending on your approach to your job search, this can be a daunting task.

The first step to creating a position/company-specific résumé is identifying a specific position that interests you at a company where you'd like to work. While this sounds easy, this is where the self-discovery we described at the beginning of the book comes in handy.

For those entering the market

The informational interviews you did and the subsequent gap analysis you conducted will help you find the right level of position you should be targeting. In this situation, informational interviews with individuals working at or who did projects at a particular company would help you identify some of the keywords and phrases you might want to highlight on your résumé. Entering the market, you will typically target junior roles, but depending on the level of education and certifications required, you might qualify for mid-tier roles.

Proper research is essential at this stage. You should be researching individuals who hold similar titles within the organization on LinkedIn to see how your skills, experience, certifications, and education align with theirs. You could also look at the different positions posted at the organization to see if they fit into a range, like "Junior," "Senior," or "Principal." This research will ensure that you are submitting for a role at the appropriate level. If not, the company may reject your application because you appear over- or under-qualified for the position. For more junior applicants, ensure that you are documenting any student roles, projects, volunteer experiences, or self-study activities, like having a home lab for learning new skills.

Once you have figured out the appropriate level for you, the next step is to tailor your résumé specifically to the keywords or phrases in the job description. There are many ways to say the same thing, so if you have a similar skill or competency or work with similar technology, use terminology straight out of the job description. If the organization utilizes an ATS, it will typically search all of the résumés based on selected keywords and bring résumés to the top that have the closest match. Once you surface at the top of this list, HR typically reviews the résumés, looking for the closest alignment to the role to determine whom to contact. As I mentioned earlier, sometimes these organizations are inundated with many applicants, so getting to the top of the list is the key to getting an interview.

For those who are mid-career

If you want to make a career pivot, do a lateral move, or start over in a new field, your approach will be slightly different. First, you want to ensure that you have conducted informational interviews to confirm that you are passionate about the role. In this situation, informational interviews with individuals working at or who worked for a particular company would help you with some of the keywords and phrases you would want to highlight in your résumé. Of course, having had work experience has its advantages, but there are some red flags you want to beware of and be prepared to answer when you get to the interview stage.

With more work experience, you will have had the opportunity to pick up job experiences and skills that new entrants to the market might not have. Be sure that you highlight that in your résumé. Laying out your experience in chronological order is the most common way of structuring your résumé. Hiring managers would look for any lengthy visible gaps between employers. If you do have gaps, there are different ways of tackling this on the résumé. You can just leave the gap without noting the hole. You might be asked to speak to the gap, so have your answer ready. You might also create a position for the gap and use a position title for it. If you choose this approach, make sure you don't create a position that never existed. Principal Consultant for You, Inc. is fine, General Manager for Big, Inc. is not if you never worked for Big, Inc. Assume the company will verify key details like job history and degrees.

Having had previous work experience, one of the things that hiring managers are looking for are signs of success in your previous roles. This section is where you can start to shine above the competition by highlighting your results and actionable steps you took to efficiently complete your initiatives. While describing your results, use as many keywords and tie in as much of the technologies listed in the job description as you can to give the hiring manager comfort that you're well-suited for the role.

> *An example*: Improved incident response times 30% by automating workflow using PowerShell and improving the alerting mechanisms.

Role-Specific Résumé

This résumé style is used more broadly than the position/company-specific résumé. While you can submit this résumé to an ATS, it shines in situations where you are bypassing the ATS. Your goal is to get this résumé directly in the hiring manager or recruiters' hands without going through the ATS. You'll find that the easiest way to do this is to avoid submitting your application online and rely instead on a member of your network delivering your résumé for you or introducing you to the hiring manager or the recruiter screening for the position.

Since your résumé is not tailored to a particular company, you want to take notes from the various informational interviews and look for similarities to the types of experiences or skills you need to highlight in your résumé. Next, look for 6-10 job postings from companies in different sectors and of varying sizes. While you can focus later more narrowly by sector and company size, at this stage you want broad exposure to job descriptions so you fully understand the critical skills that may be required. Once you have collected the different job descriptions, you should look for similarities in experience, skills, certifications, and education found in the descriptions.

For entry-level applicants, you would want to try to align your education or experiences. Ensure that you are documenting any student roles, projects, volunteer experiences, or self-study activities like having a home lab for honing or learning new skills.

For mid-career applicants, your approach will be slightly different. Hiring managers look for signs of success in your work experience, so this section is where you can start to shine above the competition by highlighting your results and the actions you took to gain those results. If possible, use the terminology and reference the technologies listed in the job description.

When it comes to effectively marketing yourself to potential employers, the résumé is one of those critical documents. My recommendation is that you always have an up-to-date role-specific résumé that you can easily craft into a company-specific résumé whenever an opportunity arises. Then, you can share your role-specific résumé with your network if you are passively looking, knowing that your company-specific résumé is a few edits away.

The Anatomy of a Cyber Résumé ~ Renee

"I attended your résumé workshop and went from receiving a paltry 1-2 calls per week to 1-2 calls per day. This is amazing!" Workshop attendee, September 2018

Résumé questions seem to be the one area that is evergreen when looking for a job. Until a person has gotten to the point of using only their LinkedIn profile, which you could substitute for your résumé, the questions continue to pour in about content, length, format, and more. As someone who has been reviewing and revising résumés for almost 20 years, the core components of a résumé remain the same, and the way I teach people to deconstruct and revise their résumés pretty much has stayed the same as well. So, I will begin by sharing the anatomy of a résumé and share my recommendations for providing résumés that produce results.

Ravi was a high-touch client. He had an open position for a DevSecOps manager, and he requested we meet, in person, to discuss his open position. The year was 2017, pre-Zoom, and I typically hosted my client meetings via conference call. I had been doing so for two years with my other clients, so it was a treat going into an office to meet with a hiring manager to discuss his role. Ravi was VP of Engineering at a small FinTech company. He had been with the company for six years and was expanding his team. He struggled to fill an open position and had deadlines that he needed to meet, so this was a priority. He had a calm, mild-mannered demeanor, and the plan was to have coffee and chat while we reviewed résumés.

We would review the résumés one by one, and he would either approve (to move to the interview stage) or decline based on a series of criteria. First, we would go over his feedback on why this person was or wasn't a fit in each case. Then, Ravi would click through the résumés on the screen, scan them quickly, and decide whether that particular résumé was in or out. Each résumé review took less than a minute. Occasionally, he would give a résumé an extra few seconds of review time for something that piqued his interest.

In one particular instance, we were going through the normal routine of résumé reviews when he paused for longer than the few extra seconds that he would typically give a résumé. We were facing each other, and I could see his eyes darting around the screen of his laptop, and for the first time since we had these meetings, he was animated. "This guy is EXACTLY what I'm looking for," he said. He went on for the next five minutes talking about this résumé. The guy's experience and the projects he had worked on aligned perfectly with the type of project that Ravi had on his team.

I chuckled and told Ravi that he had never, in my short time working with him, gotten this excited about a résumé. I also wondered if my eyes darted around the screen when I saw a résumé of a person I believe is a perfect match for a position. I wish I could have recorded this moment for all the people who ask about résumés. I have shared this story numerous times of the hiring manager who was salivating over a résumé like dog salivates over a steak.

I want all of you to have the type of résumé that gets this reaction for the job you want. You may be asking what was in that résumé that was so exciting for Ravi, the hiring manager. Was it the format? Was it his education or certifications, or summary? No, no, and no. It was that the experience detailed on the résumé matched perfectly with Ravi's current and future projects. That's all there is to it.

The résumé needs to showcase that you have the experience that aligns with the job description. If you are transitioning into security, you will need to create a résumé that shows that you have some experience that aligns with the role that you're seeking. There are some hacks to doing this that I will explain below.

The purpose of a résumé

The purpose of a résumé is to get you an interview for the job that you want. The résumé must be so exciting and enticing for a hiring manager that they will want to speak with you immediately to see if you could be a fit for their job. Anytime you receive an email, phone call, or DM regarding your résumé in response to jobs you seek, you have a great résumé and don't need to change it. If you are not receiving any calls, emails, or DMs to discuss your skills, then your résumé needs to be revised. If you are getting outreach on your résumé for jobs you do not want, your résumé needs to be revised. A résumé's purpose is NOT to get you a job. The résumé is to get you the interview, and the interview gets you the job.

The anatomy of a résumé for cybersecurity is composed of your contact info, experience, and education. I will differentiate how to structure your résumé based on the type of experience you have.

Contact info

This seems obvious to me, but I have received résumés that do not have contact information on them. I have also reviewed résumés with insufficient contact info. The information typically needed is your first and last name, cell phone, email, city, state (in the US). If you provide a home phone, you're dating yourself. I would also recommend a basic email address that is a combination of your first and last name. For example, if your email address is ilovecats@gmail.com and the hiring manager hates cats, you could be disqualified. It's best to stay neutral when job seeking, so provide a neutral email address.

Experience

Your experience should take up the majority of your résumé. It is the part of the résumé that managers and recruiters spend the most time reviewing. If I were to break a résumé into a pie chart, 70% would focus on experience.

If you are a student and have zero professional experience or internships, your coursework and additional self-directed projects will serve as your experience. Create a section in your résumé titled "Related Coursework & Cybersecurity Projects." Take the time to flesh out three to four of the courses you were most passionate about in school related to cybersecurity. Explain your coursework like you would a job. If you have volunteered to do cyber work in any capacity, add that to the résumé. This includes coursework from degree and non-degree programs. If you took a course on Cybrary or Udemy, put it on there. If you don't have any experience at all, you will need to go and gain the experience through self-directed projects and coursework.

If you are in a technology role and plan to use the transferable skills from that role in cyber, your task is to take the skills you've learned in your current tech job and align those to the future cyber role. Let's use an example. If you are in a Network Operations Center (NOC) and you would like to move into a Security Operations Center (SOC), highlight the work you're doing in the NOC that transfers to the SOC. The easiest way to do this is to find a few SOC job descriptions and align the experience that you currently have from the NOC to the SOC job description. Then, pull any verbiage from the tasks provided in the job description that you have experience doing into your résumé. You will quickly see how your skills transfer into your future cyber role.

If you are in a non-technical role and want to use your transferable skills, do the same exercise. Find your target job description, align your current experience to that job description and then use the verbiage from the job description to add to your résumé. If you have taken any cybersecurity courses or volunteered in the cybersecurity community, be sure to highlight this in the résumé.

Jason Blanchard hosts a Twitch show on reverse engineering your job search. He is an excellent resource for this.

https://www.linkedin.com/in/jasonsblanchard

Education

Your résumé should showcase your formal education and certifications. If you are a recent graduate, highlight your education at the top of your résumé. However, if your experience is strong, then the education can go to the bottom of the résumé.

Format

Keep the format, including the font, simple. I recommend this for several reasons. First, when you are applying for jobs, your résumé is likely not being read by a human initially. Instead, it goes through an applicant tracking system (ATS) for a first pass. The ATS scans your résumé and compares it to the job description. Then, many of them score the résumés based on that comparison.

The most common résumé format is chronological. This shows the most recent experience at the top of the résumé with additional experience beneath it. Stick with this format for consistency with other cybersecurity professionals.

Length

For private sector and corporate roles, here are the recommendations:

Under 5 years of experience = 1 page
Over 5 years of experience = 2 pages

For a longer-tenured professional to condense their résumé to two pages, only go back 15 years. Any experience dating back more than 15 years is likely irrelevant, and managers typically put the most weight on the more recent experience.

The résumé can be as long as it needs to be to showcase your experience for federal government and government contracting. They often require that you list all of your prior experience, and they don't want it condensed.

Additional items

List volunteer work, affiliations, and anything else you'd like to share that give your résumé more dimension and show relevant non-work-related aspects of your life at the very bottom of the résumé.

In conclusion, there are many hacks to make your résumé attractive to hiring managers. By displaying the right experience, you can have hiring managers excited over your résumé and ready to hire you as the perfect solution to their cybersecurity problem.

Resources:

- Jason Blanchard/BanjoCrashland is a Twitch show providing free résumé and career advice.
  https://m.twitch.tv/banjocrashland
- Justin Jones hosts frequent, free online hiring events on LinkedIn mostly targeted to military veterans.
  https://www.linkedin.com/in/justin-jones-cism-pmp-27155042
- Jobscan helps you optimize your résumé to get past the applicant tracking systems (ATS)
  https://www.jobscan.co/

Articles on résumé writing
- https://www.monster.com/career-advice/article/sample-resume-information-security-specialist
- https://news.clearancejobs.com/cyber-security-resume-sample/

Chapter 7 – Key Points and Recommended Actions

The following is a quick summary of the key points from this chapter:

- Your résumé is an indispensable document constructed to get you an interview. The interview gets you the job.
- Ensure that your résumé provides the essential information for the recruiter and hiring manager.
- Be purposeful about how you build your résumé. It is common to have several résumés, highlighting different aspects of your career and capabilities.
- Proofread your résumé and ask someone else with good writing skills to take a second look. Nothing will deselect you for a job faster than misspelled words and poor grammar.
- Assume that potential employers will verify all statements of fact on your résumé.

Chapter 8

Searching for a Cybersecurity Job

Introduction

The job search outcome is more often determined by the strategy used than the effort put forth. In this chapter, we provide various techniques for your job search that align with the phase of your cybersecurity career. Your experience, whether you are transitioning and where you are in your career development, are all factors that should inform how you go about your search.

At the beginning of your search, we encourage you to have an open mind. Don't narrow your focus too soon. As all of us have said repeatedly, this field is still evolving, and the needs continue to grow. Their need is your opportunity. Once you narrow down the perfect role for you, you can dig into the details like salary range, requirements, and expected experience. The job description will give you the details needed to tweak your résumé along with what you need to submit for the next step.

We also provide strategies for transitioning within an organization, coming directly from college, and coming from another industry. Not every technique will apply to everyone or work in every situation. Integrate these strategies into your approach to optimize your outcome.

Gary created another real-world example by conducting an online job search and breaking down with snippets of the search output how he analyses the search results. He points out what to look for and how to interpret the results so you can refine your search and home in on the perfect job for you.

Chris shares his secrets for matching your skills and experience to the right level of job. Most employers are looking for a little stretch – they don't want the proverbial revolving door of candidates who master the job in weeks and move on. It is counter-intuitive until Chris unpacks it for you, but it turns out to be spot on.

Renee organizes her advice around the job seeker's entry point. She treats college graduates and individuals transitioning in the middle of their career differently because their needs, expectations and abilities can vary greatly.

As you read these three essays, you'll spot reflections of yourself in all three. Combining these techniques into a unified toolkit and then using the best tools for you at whatever your career stage gives you a competitive advantage in your hunt.

Searching for Your First Cybersecurity Job ~ Gary

In recent discussions with groups of veterans and civilians looking for their first jobs in private industry, I told them about my career in IT and cybersecurity. Many of the men and women I spoke to at these events were interested in learning how to search for a cybersecurity job. Their questions are the basis for this next chapter. As we begin, this information should not be viewed as a how-to guide for the experienced security practitioner who is already working in the cyber career field. Instead, it is a collection of insights for anyone currently performing a technical or cybersecurity job search that needs some help. Hopefully, this information will make that search easier for you.

What information do you have?

When beginning your job hunt, remember it's all about gathering information. You should first review whom you know. Yes, that's correct. I am not recommending using a computer first but instead, using your network. If you are looking for a job in the technology or cybersecurity industry, one of the best ways to find out who is hiring, what technology is on the rise, and what experience employers want is by asking peers for their advice.

If you are new to the technology or cybersecurity field, you can get this information from professional organizations such as ISSA, ISACA, InfraGard, OWASP, ISC2, and IAPP. Many of these organizations have chapters worldwide and sponsor monthly meetings where members come together to have a meal, hear a speaker, or conduct an event such as "capture the flag." Another part of the information-gathering process is to research the various positions in the field you want to join so you understand the educational, technical, and work requirements you will have to meet. An excellent reference for cybersecurity is the National Initiative for

Cybersecurity Careers and Studies' (NICCS) NICE Cybersecurity Workforce Framework.[31]

Searching for your job, cast a wide net!

Assume you have now gathered some information. You have spoken with peers, mentors, and friends. After reviewing the NICE framework, you feel your experience and training match well with the "Security Analyst" job description (this is the example I have selected for the chapter). Now it's time to use your computer. and Start by using a search engine to cast a wide net for information and then narrowing that view with specific job boards. Let's look at what I get with the wide net approach searching for "information security analyst."

I found generic data about the occupation with the first search, which is useful if this is a new career field for you. I quickly noticed some interesting information on the pay range, and I can see the questions other people have asked about this role. Plus, I can see other websites listed, such as the Bureau of Labor, where you could go and read up on this occupation, and you can see similar professions at the bottom of the search results that you may not have thought about when you started your search.

Something worth noting here is the pay range for this job is much higher than average pay. When jobs have pay ranges that are higher than a specific norm, it is because of some unique requirements for that role. This requirement could be a specific technical skill or experience with a particular tool. It's essential that in your search you note what you find for recommended skills, education, and certifications, and what a typical day is like for someone in this type of position. Ensure that you build a well-rounded picture. Don't be

---

[31] https://niccs.us-cert.gov/workforce-development

afraid to go back to the people you spoke to in your first step and validate the information you have collected.

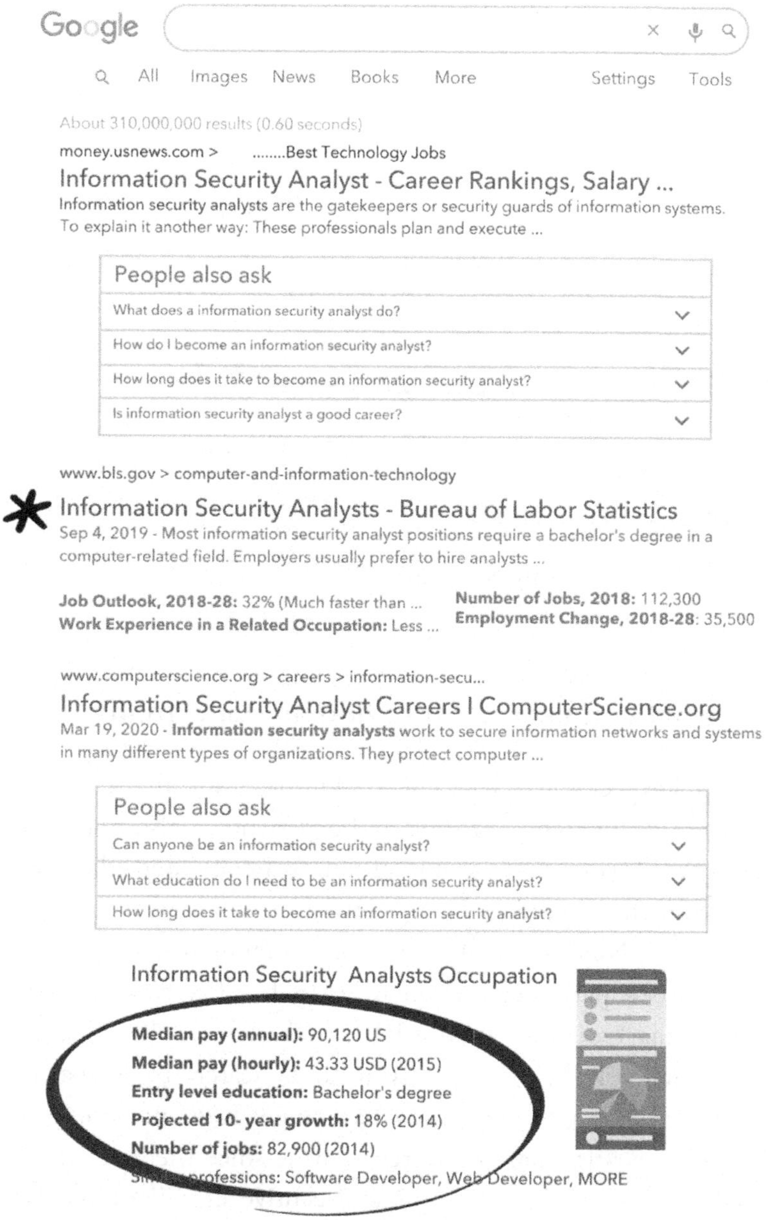

Figure 8.1 Search 1 of 6

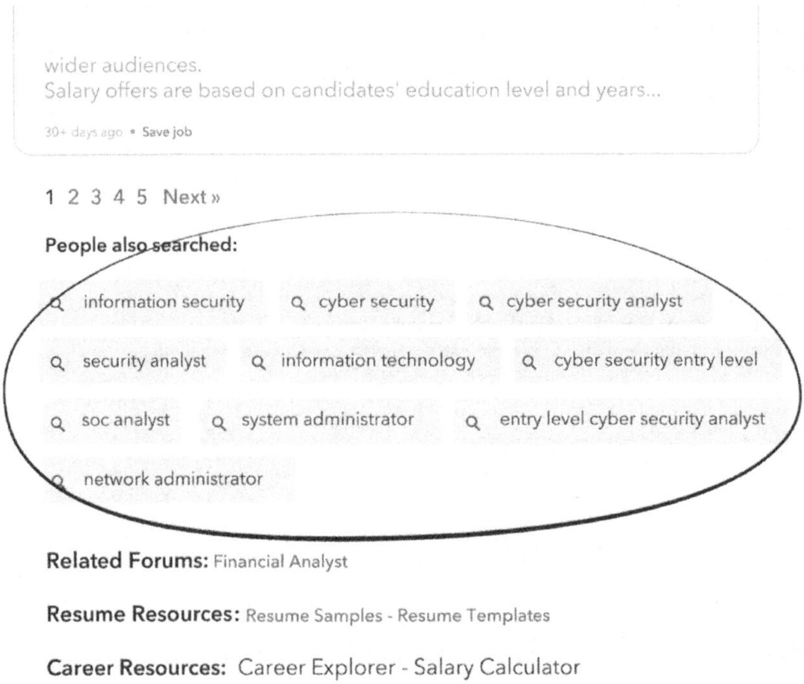

wider audiences.
Salary offers are based on candidates' education level and years...

30+ days ago • Save job

1 2 3 4 5 Next »

People also searched:

- information security
- cyber security
- cyber security analyst
- security analyst
- information technology
- cyber security entry level
- soc analyst
- system administrator
- entry level cyber security analyst
- network administrator

Related Forums: Financial Analyst

Resume Resources: Resume Samples - Resume Templates

Career Resources: Career Explorer - Salary Calculator

Figure 8.2 Search 2 of 6

Narrow what you search for to find an opportunity

By this step, I expect you to have collected information about specific job types you feel match your skills and experience. I also hope you have completed your first group of job searches, and the data returned from these searches have helped to validate some of your career decisions. Now comes the fun part: searching for an open job listing for the occupation you selected. To do this effectively, I would recommend that you start with a job search website. Using a job search website will help you narrow your search to a specific geographical location or a required pay range. I am not going to recommend any particular job search website since there are many you can choose from, plus don't forget executive sites like LinkedIn also offer the ability to search for jobs.

To continue our example, I have searched for an Information Security Analyst position in the San Diego area on a job search website. From the search results, I can see specific job positions currently open in San Diego, and I can see the estimated monthly pay ranges for some of them. An important point to remember from the picture I have included for this step is most job websites will have advanced search parameters. "Advanced Search" will allow you to create filters so you can search for a particular job title, pay range, location, or part-time/full-time. I mention this because you can save these unique searches, and if the website has the feature, you can set the search to run daily, weekly, or monthly and email you the results.

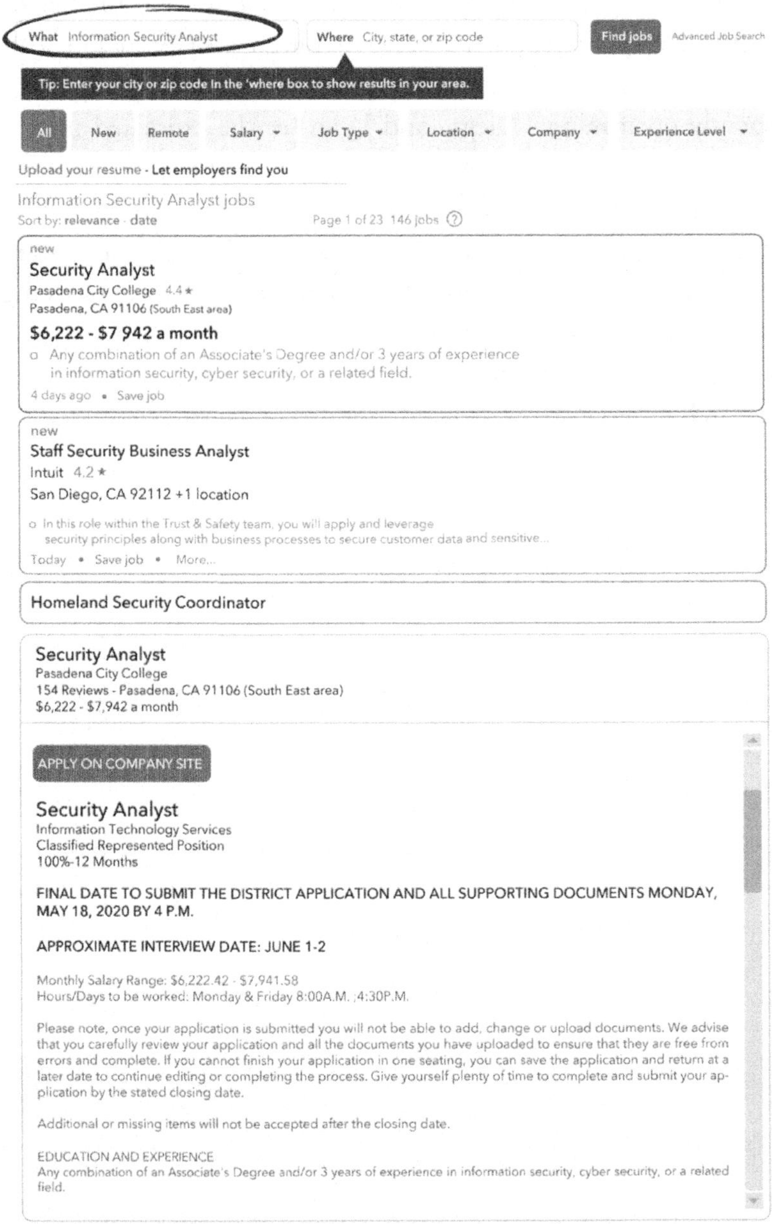

Figure 8.3 Search 3 of 6

I think I have found a job

This step is where you narrow your search to a specific job opening that you feel matches your skills, experience, and education. The example we will continue to use for this step is an Information Security Analyst position in San Diego for the employer San Diego State University. I want to point something out here. Don't be surprised how confusing job requirements for a position can be. For the rest of this chapter, I will help you decipher the criteria for the job I have selected, and hopefully this process will provide you with the insight to do it yourself.

Now, back to the position at San Diego State University that I selected for our example. In image below, you can see the official job title and that the position is full-time and reports to the Chief Information Security Officer.

Reading the job description, you can see some of the requirements (investigating, researching, logging, and tracking) expected daily of someone in this position. This information is important because if you apply and interview for this position, you will get questions in the job interview about the abilities or experience you have to meet these requirements.

Finally, under the "Education and Experience" section, you should note one sentence I underlined because the employer specifically calls out skills/experiences that are a prerequisite. This means you need to have them before applying for the job, so if you have them definitely include them in your résumé when applying for the position. Note, they state they expect you would get this experience from having a bachelor's degree, but they don't make that mandatory. This leaves you room if you have job experience instead of a degree. Look for that opening if you lack the degree but have extensive experience. Many in the military have the experience, so don't be afraid to leverage it.

Job Title:
7149 Information Security Analyst (Operating Systems Analyst - Career),
Information Technology Security Office

Appointment Type:
Probationary

Time Base:
Full-Time

Date Posted:
January 16, 2020

Closing Date:
Open until filled

Benefits Link:
CSUEU (Unit 2, 5, 7, 9)

Link to Apply Online:
https://bfa.sdsu.edu/hr/jobs/job-opportunities.aspx

Campus Employment Homepage:
http://jobs.sdsu.edu

Description:
Position Summary

Reporting to the Chief Information Security Officer, the Information Security Analyst will support the goals and objectives of San Diego State University security program which include security incident response, threat hunting, risk identification, and risk analysis. This position plays an integral role in investigating, researching, logging, tracking, and following up on security incidents, as well as, legal and regulatory requirements.

Additionally, the incumbent will continuously assist with activities required to increase SDSU's awareness of information security practices, and safeguards. This includes enhancing the related information for security program policies, standards, procedures, guidelines, coordinated education and awareness.

For more information regarding Information Technology Security Office, please click here: https://itsdsu.edu/security

This is a full-time (1.0 time-base), benefits eligible, permanent (probationary) position. This position is designated exempt under FLSA and is not eligible for overtime compensation. Standard work hours are Monday - Friday, 8:00 a.m. to 4:30 p.m., but may vary based on operational needs.
Education and Experience

To enter this classification, a basic foundation of knowledge and skills in operating systems programs, maintenance, and systems administration features is prerequisite. This foundation would normally be obtained through a bachelor's degree, preferably in computer science, mathematics, or a related technical field, or equivalent technical training and/or experience.

Figure 8.4 Search 4 of 6

Don't forget your soft skills

Now we are into the core part of a job description, the actual qualifications and skills you are expected to have if you apply. I want you to first focus on the word I have circled in figure 8.5, "Preferred." Why did I focus on this word? It's important because it means the qualifications and skills listed below aren't mandatory; they are a shopping list for the employer. They are looking for someone that has most of those skills. I like interviews where it's "preferred" because now you can tell your value story of how the skills and experience you have make you the best candidate.

There are a couple of other things I want you to notice and think about. The first is the call out for an "Information Security Certification." Notice they don't state what certification, they just expect you to have one, and the good news is you aren't limited to a specific cert. The other important things I want you to note are the soft skills they expect you to possess.

I focus on this because it is critical. I can guarantee that if you make it to the interview stage, you will be asked to give examples of how you have used ingenuity or how you have troubleshot a problem. It would be best if you were prepared for the hiring manager to ask you in the interview about your approach to solving a hypothetical problem and explain why you made specific decisions. You need to understand that they are looking for a good fit for their team, so it's more than just technical skills. Come prepared and be ready. They have given you their roadmap for the interview, and now you know how to read it.

(Preferred) Qualifications and Specialized Skills

- Experience designing and implementing security solutions
- Information Security Certification
- Working knowledge of Risk and control frameworks and process improvement models, and ability to analyze data and make recommendations on risks and security issues
- Data-related security principles and safeguard measures
- Familiarity with security compliance standards such as ISO 27000 series, NISI 800-53
- Experience with Windows and Linux operating systems and their security framework
- Penetration testing of applications and infrastructure
- Possess ingenuity to solve technical problems with creative methods and thinking
- Excellent written and verbal skills and the demonstrated competence to effectively present information in either format
- Excellent organizational skills
- Cloud computing - the risks and benefits of using a vendor's remote servers to store, manage and process an organization's data
- Excellent troubleshooting and problem-solving skills
- Working knowledge of security issues, techniques and implications across computer platforms
- Proficiency in scripting languages and multiple programming, such as scripting and/or Programming languages (PHP, PowerShell, Python, Java, C/C++, .NET)
- Experience with web application security testing, web application security issues and mitigation measures
- Common Internet standards and protocols, such as TCP/IP, computer networking, routing and switching - an understanding of the fundamentals: the language, protocol and functioning of the Internet
- Knowledge of intrusion detection and prevention systems, and IDS/IPS principles and tools
- Security system analysis, development, application programming, and database analysis

Figure 8.5 Search 5 of 6

Check the final details

To recap, we have found a job that we want to apply for, and we feel we have many of the preferred qualifications and skills. In this final step, I want you to focus on the last section at the end of a job description. For this example, Information Security Analyst at San

Diego State University, the final part is labeled "Compensation and Benefits." In this section, what is essential here will be things like the ones I have underlined. This includes the starting salary, when the review of the résumés will begin and end, and if the position requires drug testing, background checks, or work authorization. Do not forget to review this section; if you submit your résumé late, you will never get the chance to interview.

Compensation and Benefits

Starting salary upon appointment not expected to exceed $8333 per month. CSU Classification Salary Range: $4,372 - $10,792 per month. Salary placement is determined by the education, experience, and qualifications the candidate brings to the position, internal equity, and the hiring department's fiscal resources.

San Diego State University offers a rich benefits package that constitutes a major portion of total compensation. For more information regarding SDSU benefits, please click here: https://bfa.sdsu.edu/hr/jobs/benefits

Supplemental Information

Initial review of the required application materials including cover letters and resumes, will begin on January 23, 2020. To receive full consideration, apply by January 22, 2020. The position will remain open until filled.

The person holding this position is considered a 'mandated reporter' under the California Child Abuse and Neglect Reporting Act and is required to comply with the requirements set forth in CSU Executive Order 1083 as a condition of employment.

San Diego State University is not a sponsoring agency for staff or management positions (e.g., H-18 visa). Applicants must currently be authorized to work in the United States on a full-time basis. Offers of employment are contingent upon the presentation of documents at (Demonstrate a person's identity and authorization to work in the United States, which are consistent with the provisions of the immigration Reform and Control Act.

A background check (including a criminal records check) must he completed satisfactorily before any candidate can be offered a position with the CSU. Failure to satisfactorily complete the background check may affect the application status of applicants or continued employment of current CSU employees who apply for the position.

SDSU is a smoke-free campus. For more information, please click here: https://smokefree.sdsu.edu/

SDSU is an equal opportunity employer and does not discriminate against persons on the basis of race, religion, national origin, sexual orientation, gender, gender identity and expression, marital status, age, disability, pregnancy, medical condition, or covered veteran status.

Applicants with disabilities and applicants who require assistance completing an application may contact Meracle Cothron at 619 - 594-1139.

Figure 8.6 Search 6 of 6

In closing, I hope I have given you some necessary information to get you started applying for positions and some insight into understanding the requirements of any job you select. One last note to help you with this process is I recommend keeping a spreadsheet that lists each job you have applied for with the contact information and what résumé you submitted. This spreadsheet will allow you to track which positions are still active, which filled, and which were "Did not meet requirements." Approach this focused on the end goal of finding your job and take not getting a position as a learning opportunity rather than a negative. Decide if you need to refine your approach, move to the next job opening, and keep trying. Don't forget to continue to actively talk with your network throughout this process, and don't be afraid to ask the community for help.

Searching for Your Cybersecurity Job ~ Chris

By now, you are ready to search for your cybersecurity role; you have a solid foundation of skills, have a reliable network, and a stellar résumé that will have recruiters and hiring managers ringing your phone off the hook. But where do you start?

Searching for cybersecurity roles might seem like trying to find a needle in a haystack, especially to those just trying to get into the field. Job descriptions can be daunting, and many of the items listed might not even really align with the actual requirements of the role. This has been the experience of many of the guests on *Breaking into Cybersecurity*, and I've experienced this too. Some of these misalignments may stem from:

- a mismatch between the requirements communicated from hiring managers to recruiters
- copy/paste job descriptions
- job descriptions based on the skills and competencies of the outgoing resource
- hiring managers wish list of skills, which might not align with the compensation expectations of candidates

Based on observations and job search tips from our own experience and that of our guests, applying for positions where you are highly passionate about the role and meeting 50-60% of the requirements seems to strike an excellent balance for a couple of reasons.

First, applying for a role in which you have all of the listed experiences and skills is likely to leave you bored in the position in a relatively short time. While some might like the stability of this type of role, you will likely get bored and want to quickly leave for a more advanced position if you are looking to grow in your career. Hiring managers also recognize this drawback to hiring fully qualified candidates for entry-level jobs and will sometimes consider candidates who meet all the requirements as overqualified.

This problem is certainly not the case for all jobs. For example, hiring managers for contract or project roles, which might be limited in responsibilities, contract term, or minimum requirements for the contract, might need to fill these roles as described for their clients. Typically, government clients are very strict with their contract experience, education, and certification requirements, much more so than commercial companies.

Second, hiring for internal roles, or looking for long-term employees, usually boils down to finding the best candidate with a blend of the requested skills within the requested budget. Trying to balance all of these requirements is why not having all the listed requirements can be attractive to hiring managers. Depending on the geographical job market, a candidate who has all the noted experience, skills, competencies, education, and certifications will likely demand a salary far surpassing the budgeted salary for a role. While some very large enterprises can certainly pay at or above market to get the exact person they want, that is often not the case for small and medium-sized companies.

It will be up to you to sell the value you bring to the company with a mix of experience, education, and certification. Selling value can be done by demonstrating your passion, continuous learning, and drive to excel, combined with other factors such as soft skills to set yourself apart from the competition.

Know what you want and don't want to do

While it might be tempting to say that you will take any job in cybersecurity just to get in, this strategy will leave you frustrated, possibly burned out, and looking for a new role sooner than you'd like. As recommended in previous chapters, figuring out what you do and do not want to do in cybersecurity is just as critical a step in your job hunt as the interviews. Understanding your desired job requirements should come from the informational interviews from Chapter 2 (Finding your Passion) and Chapter 3 (Skills

Assessments). They will be critical to help you discover more about the pros and cons of the different roles and how they align with your passions and skillsets.

I am not saying that you can't just take any job to get in, but if you do, there is a particular approach and mindset to be successful. First, if you plan to do this, make sure that the goal of this first role is for learning and on-the-job training, not necessarily the pleasure of the position. This educational approach can be challenging due to the time and cost commitment, so decide if you are up for the challenge before jumping into it. Secondly, make a timed commitment for yourself on how long you plan to dedicate yourself to learning this new job. I would recommend starting with a 12–18-month trial minimum to dedicate yourself to learning all aspects of a particular role.

As stated, knowing what you don't want to do is just as important as knowing what you want to do. Even if you get your foot in the door by taking an educational opportunity, you do not want to be doing something that goes against your natural strengths, ethics, or personal goals. These types of positions tend to destroy your drive, burn you out, and even create a disdain for the field.

Know where you want to go in the future, not just right now

It might be easy to choose an already-established position as your first role if you are a new or transitioning entrant to the field. Still, I would recommend researching the field to see if you can identify trends or new skills which seem likely to become important in the future. Then, finding a role to learn these skills while on the job will be a worthwhile investment. For example, five to 10 years ago, the skill set of machine learning algorithms seemed cutting edge and futuristic. Today they are becoming common for developers and a new requirement for some senior-level roles within the cybersecurity field. Another example of such an evolution is cloud computing; 10

to 15 years ago, it was a novelty. Today cloud is a foundational requirement for many companies, where many startups never own any existing physical infrastructure themselves.

Some other steps that are helpful in career planning are your imagination and goal setting. I suggest making your goals "SMART," which stands for Specific, Measurable, Achievable, Relevant, and Time-bound. Imagination as a tool is the visualization of longer-term desires that provide a more extensive guide to your career. A quick example of the differences between these two tools is that a goal could be to "Study for and complete the certification testing for the Security+ Certification in the next 90 days," while an imagined goal could be "Become a CISO in five to 10 years." I would highly encourage you to create a vision for your career and let that roadmap be your guide throughout your career. This process also allows you to work backward and develop specific goals that will move you toward achieving those dreams.

Know where to look and the best ways to apply

There are so many different ways to look and apply for roles, so I am going to deep dive into the more common ones so we can look at the pros and cons:

Job Boards (Such as CareerBuilder, Indeed, Glassdoor, Craigslist) – Job boards are websites where companies post available jobs or job openings that have been scraped from different sources to facilitate easier searching and application to posted roles. The fact that job boards aggregate listings from many companies allow candidates to use these sites as a one-stop-shop. Some job boards allow applicants to apply for the role using the site, while others will redirect you to the company job portal. The downside to these sites is that there could be duplication of job postings (scraping from the same post somewhere else) or stale and closed positions filled by the hiring companies that appear active on the job boards.

Company Job Portals – Company job portals are a specific portion of a companies' website focused on attracting talent and highlighting open roles for the particular organization. These often provide the most current listing of open positions at the company and how to apply for these roles. The only downside to using this approach is that to apply to several different companies, you will have to go to each of their sites individually. However, from my experience, it is no less effective than using an aggregator. It is just more time-intensive as it is not a one-stop approach.

Social Media – Often, hiring companies will directly post open positions or high-priority positions on their social media profiles, typically on LinkedIn or Twitter. This usually indicates that there is a more urgent need for those roles. Hiring managers or employees on teams with an open role might also help recruit by posting links to open positions to broaden the search's reach.

> *Pro Tip: Interact directly with the hiring managers or individuals on the hiring team for more insights on the role. This direct contact can also improve your chance of getting selected for an interview. This could be as simple as reaching out to them directly, responding to their posts, or posting topics that might interest them and sharing the link privately with them.*

Using your network for referrals – Having a good network of connections will allow you to use this network to amplify the effects of your search. For example, these individuals can help you identify roles, connect you with hiring managers and recruiters, and even help you better prepare for interviews.

> *Pro Tip: Connections or their connections sometimes can have access to a hidden job market of unposted roles or roles pending final approvals, but they are already looking for candidates.*

Balancing your approach

The job search process does not always yield results overnight and based on my experience, will frequently take a minimum of four to eight weeks. You need to be aware of the extended timeframe in which job searches occur because it can be a mentally exhausting process. There is also a feeling of monotony in the job search process because you are repeatedly doing the same thing, often without seeing any results from those actions. Here is an approach based on my experience that I think will help you balance your efforts across the significant sources of leads:

- Spend 20% of your time focused on company job portals, job boards, and social networking sites like LinkedIn

- Spend 50% of your time focused on networking with new and existing contacts, building relationships, and providing value to your network

- Spend 30% of your time focused on continuous learning and integrating current events into the talking points of your interviews to show relevant experience

As mentioned in earlier chapters, since hiring managers and recruiters are often inundated with résumés that come through their ATS from job boards or their company portal, you need to find ways to stand out from the pack. Unfortunately, while formatting your résumé to be ATS-friendly can help, it is not a sure-fire way to get the hiring manager's attention. For this reason, I highly recommend focusing a lot of your time on networking. Connect with new and existing contacts, build relationships, provide value to your network, and invest in continuous learning and integrating current events into the talking points of your interviews to show relevant experience.

How to Search for a Job ~ Renee

"I've applied to 400 jobs online, and I can't get an interview."

"Getting a job in cybersecurity is so hard. I'm so frustrated, and I don't know what to do."

"I'm quitting looking for a job in cybersecurity. I'm going back to my old field."

"It took over 30 interviews for me to get a job."

For the past few years, I have received daily messages like this in my inbox asking for help breaking into the industry. I encourage aspiring cyber professionals to stop doing what isn't working and to take a different approach. Based on where they are in their careers and professional experience, I provide varying methods for searching for a job in cybersecurity. Trust me, networking with people in the field is the best way to land your first job.

There is a famous quote that says, "bloom where you are planted." This quote's meaning is to be fruitful and make the most out of the opportunities in front of you. Many times, people overlook easy pathways into security by not leveraging their current situation. These approaches will give you ideas for finding a job in the industry using the resources you currently have at your fingertips.

Searching for a job as a traditional college student without experience

If you are a traditional college student who is attending a full-time college program and not working at all, there are several resources that you can use to look for an opportunity.

The first is to utilize your school's office of career services. In most universities, there is a career services office that provides resources for their students. These services include résumé writing workshops, interview strategies classes, and a plethora of job opportunities for current students and recent grads. Additionally, there is typically a student portal that provides job opportunities. Universities also tend to run their career fairs with employers who pay to participate. Career fairs are an awesome way to start looking for an opportunity as the employers are specifically looking for students from your university or program. Often, these employers partner with the college or university to have the students and recent grads begin work at their organizations.

Employers sometimes also sponsor events at schools they partner with. For example, employers will host pizza parties, career discussions, informational events to showcase their company, and other events to raise awareness of their company to students. You might also get some cool swag.

Most universities host at least one career fair per semester. More often than not, they host a multitude of career fairs. Some are more general and have companies from all industries seeking students and recent grads from various majors. Other career fairs are more focused and may only invite students from specific programs. For example, there may be an "all-IT" career fair where employers only look for students studying IT and related majors. There are also career fairs targeted to graduate students, and those also have jobs that may require an advanced degree.

Anyone who is a college student should be aggressively utilizing the office of career services' resources. Your tuition is paying for these resources, so it is the first place to start as a college student.

The next place to learn about opportunities is through your college professors. Years ago, when working as a campus recruiter, I often worked with hiring managers who were adjunct professors. They would share opportunities with their students and encourage students to apply to various internships and jobs. I'm currently working on an open position right now that requires an advanced specialized Ph.D. The hiring manager provided a list of professors to reach out to who might know students they could recommend for the role. You should definitely connect with your professors and ask if they are aware of any opportunities. Remember that professors also have colleagues and friends in the industry, and if they don't know of an open position directly, they may have friends who do. Ask them to keep an eye out for jobs for you.

Another way to learn about job opportunities while you are in college is to join professional organizations that align with your major. Again, these are often sponsored by a professor or department head. If you join and volunteer to be a leader in one of these professional organizations, you immediately gain access to more professionals in the field and access to jobs. In addition, these groups tend to share job openings with their student members to provide entry-level opportunities.

As shared in other chapters throughout this book, use social media like LinkedIn to build a network of professionals in the area of security where you'd like to work. Join online forums and participate in webinars and other activities to gain visibility and get in front of people who could potentially hire you or refer you to an opportunity.

Mid-career transitioners and non-traditional college students

Have you ever heard of the saying, "the grass is always greener on the other side of the fence?" When listening to career transitioners, I think of this phrase when they talk about their struggles getting a job in cybersecurity. Some career changers are in massive organizations where they can leverage their expertise in that company as well as the experiences they've built over the years to break into cybersecurity.

If you go back in time 15 to 20 years, almost everyone who had a cybersecurity job got that job by transitioning within their organization to take on the role. Many of the people were systems admins, network admins, and software developers. Very often, they volunteered or were "volun-told" into these roles. They brought the experiences they had already had and utilized those skills to succeed in their new cybersecurity jobs.

Today, this still happens, and it has happened across more departments than just IT. Almost every CISO I have ever met has transitioned into their role from somewhere outside of the cybersecurity department. In addition, many security leaders have come from varying backgrounds in organizations. I have worked with many cybersecurity professionals who have come out of various departments, including operations, internal audit, sales and marketing, communications, finance and accounting, customer service, procurement, and HR. These individuals have leveraged the experiences that they had in their former departments and used transferable skills to break into cybersecurity in their current companies.

As I mentioned, I co-host the *Breaking into Cybersecurity* podcast and LinkedIn Live series. On many of our #CISO Thursdays shows, our co-hosts Naomi Buckwalter and James Azar describe how they have transitioned into the field and give tips for career transitioners. In addition, Chris Foulon, my co-host, and co-author, has often shared his transition story and shared strategies.

Naomi gave a great step-by-step plan to gain cybersecurity exposure within your company. First, she recommended that a person reach out to their cybersecurity department and volunteer to assist by being a "cybersecurity champion" in your current department. A "cybersecurity champion" is someone who takes cybersecurity tips back to your current department and shares information on how the department can keep the company's data safe. They also may be the liaison between their department and the cybersecurity department. By volunteering for this type of project, the career transitioner can show that they are assets to the cybersecurity team. They can also share that they are taking classes, certifications, or getting a degree in the field.

By volunteering your time while you are in your current role, there are multiple wins for you and the organization:

1. You can gain knowledge and experience in cybersecurity and get insight into your colleagues' challenges. You are also able to share best practices from the cybersecurity department with your current department.

2. If your department is frustrated with the cybersecurity recommendations, you can take those frustrations back to the cybersecurity team.

3. You can also be a cybersecurity champion, sharing why your department should follow the cybersecurity protocols and explaining the consequences of not doing so.

On a recent video conference call, I met with three women who were breaking into cybersecurity. They all are career transitioners working full-time jobs while attending a cybersecurity master's degree program. I asked them to share their current full-time roles and what they intended to do once they had their degrees. Two of them were in healthcare and were interested in pivoting into security with their healthcare backgrounds. The other was in the automotive industry.

I shared with the group that their strategy could be to take Naomi's advice and look within their current companies to build their skills and gain experience, if possible. I shared the formula Naomi outlined above since they had been trying to find roles outside of their organizations in cybersecurity with no luck. I explained to them that they should leverage the skills they currently have to pivot in their organizations. If there is no opportunity for a job in the organization, at least they would have gained some additional skills and experience to be used on their résumés.

They had not thought of utilizing their current skills and underestimated the value they already brought to their current organizations. I shared that they should use their experience and skills and the education that their companies were shouldering to pave the way for themselves within the company. As James Azar pointed out in a recent podcast, this must align with its growth and cross-training culture. If the company is opposed to employees in one department volunteering for another department, be cognizant of that. Ask your manager if it's ok. You won't want to put your current situation in jeopardy while you're pivoting into a new profession.

Additional ways to search for a job with no degree or job

If you are unemployed and don't have a degree, here are some ways to search for a cyber job while gaining actual hands-on experience. By participating in cybersecurity competitions such as capture the flag (CTFs) and bug bounty programs, you will draw the attention of hiring leaders who often attend these competitions to recruit.

As described in startacybercareer.com, CTFs are a great way to gain real-world experience and land a job. I can share my own experience as a recruiter. When searching for talent for a specific position, the hiring manager asked that I visit various CTF websites to reach out to some of the winners. The leader wasn't concerned with the college degree or years of experience of the participants. He just wanted to speak with people who ranked highly in the various CTF competitions.

Bug bounty programs are also a place to gain experience and gain the attention of hiring authorities. Many organizations have payouts for people to find bugs in their websites and software. There are large corporations and small businesses that have these programs. There are also bug bounty organizations like HackerOne and Hack The Box where people can get their start doing bug bounties.

In summary, there are many ways to search for a cybersecurity job as a new person breaking into the field. With the options above, I hope to see people stay away from general, large job sites and do more networking and security activities to raise the awareness of hiring leaders. That is a more exciting way to get your first opportunity in cybersecurity!

Resources:

- https://securediversity.org/how-to-gain-practical-cyber-experience/
- https://startacybercareer.com/how-to-get-cyber-security-experience/
- https://www.hackthebox.eu/
- https://www.hackerone.com/

Chapter 8 – Key Points and Recommended Actions

The following is a quick summary of the key points from this chapter:

- Searching for a job begins with your network. You won't be working for a computer, so don't start with a computer. Instead, use your network to gather intel and let the world know you are looking.
- Be thoughtful and open-minded. Remember that you'll be spending years working for this company and with these people. You want to love what you're doing, and you want to be in continual growth.
- When it's time to use computers, search for opportunities and gather information about prospective employers, bosses, and co-workers, be methodical. There is a huge array of tools, including search engines, websites, job boards and social media. Dig deep and take notes.
- Learn to recognize the indirect messages. What is the meaning behind how the job description was written? What are they telling you and not telling you?
- Don't fall in love with a job too early, and don't shut out an opportunity too quickly. Instead, channel your enthusiasm by balancing your immediate and long-terms needs with those of the hiring company.

Chapter 9

The Cybersecurity Job Interview

Introduction

The purpose of this chapter is to walk you through what a cybersecurity job interview could look like and provide you with information on the types of questions to expect and what you should ask your potential employer.

Your first impression in the interview is significant; it sets the stage for the whole process, so do your homework. You do not want to lose a possible chance to work at a great company by coming across as unprofessional or unprepared.

The interview should be a two-way process. They will ask you questions, and it's just as essential for you to vet them. Approach your interviews with the intention to gather knowledge about the potential employer that you cannot get from the job description. To succeed at vetting your potential employer, you'll want to have a list of questions ready to ask your interviewer.

This chapter focuses on preparing you for that interview and provides information on the different types of interviews you may encounter in your cybersecurity job search. Throughout our careers in cybersecurity, the one constant we've seen regarding job interviews is that every interview has been different. And because each company approaches how they hire differently, we decided to focus on steps you can use to conduct your research for the interview. Doing this research will help reduce your nervousness, and hopefully, you will be more professional and at ease answering their questions.

As Gary, Chris, and Renee will tell you, interview preparation consists of research (on the company, the interviewer, and the job), analyzing the job description, and preparing the questions you're going to ask.

The old saying goes, "You never get a second chance to make a first impression." Therefore, you need a methodology to prepare and a process to follow during the interview. Following this process provides the potential employer with the information they need to make their decision. You also become educated about the company's needs, people, and culture. As a result, you will be able to decide if the prospective company is right for you.

Preparing for Your Cybersecurity Job Interview ~ Gary

A friend I am mentoring recently asked how she should prepare for a job interview. She is like many of the new practitioners coming into the cybersecurity community. She had little experience in technology but is making a career shift and had heard that cybersecurity job interviews could be stressful. Upon hearing the request, I was confused because I knew she had already applied for jobs recently. However, upon further clarification, she admitted the process had not gone very well, and she needed help.

I had never thought about the methodology I have developed to prepare for information technology or cybersecurity-related job interviews. I have worked in both fields, and to me, they are both just technical interviews. But I now understand how daunting they can be for people who have never worked in this field before. For the sake of our discussion, I will focus on how I prepare for a cybersecurity interview. But understand that the process I describe is interchangeable and can be used for technology interviews as well. Hopefully, you will gain some insight into my preparation process, and it will help you prepare for your next job interview.

In Chapter 8, I provided you with a process for searching and applying for a job in cybersecurity. Now we come to the next stage, when you have completed your research and applied for several jobs, and one of them has contacted you for an interview. Of course, now maybe you are nervous – you will need to speak to strangers and explain to them how you are the right person for this position. But that is ok because our discussion here will focus on preparing you for that meaningful conversation.

Do your research

After talking with the company's HR team or external recruiter about an interview, the next step is to research the company. When you were initially applying for the job, you may have done some cursory research, but with your upcoming interview it's time to get serious. To begin, I search for news articles about the company. I will typically go back five years. I want to see both the good and bad news reported about a company, and I am interested in any trends. I look for mergers and acquisitions, new services or products, and executives who have recently joined or departed. I also will research their financials if they are available. I want to know how well the business is doing, what markets they compete in, what regulations or lawsuits currently impact them, and finally, what people are saying about the company. This research provides a more well-rounded picture of the company and will help you better understand their culture and whether you want to be a part of it. Do not neglect this step; it is critically important.

Usually, when scheduling an interview with a company, you will also be told who will conduct the interview. I highly recommend writing those names and titles down because you will want to research your interviewer(s). Think of it as getting to know some potential new friends. Again, I would search for articles that they may have written or news about them and the company. I would also review social media and look at their content, posts, friends, and groups. This research helps humanize the interviewer and reduces your stress because they become just an ordinary person. It will also give you some points of interest to talk about in the interview to relate to each other. All of this makes it easier to make your case that you are the best candidate for the position.

Researching both the company and interviewer(s) is essential because, as one who has hired many people over the years, I can tell you they will research each potential candidate before they sit down and talk to you, so come prepared. If you have done your homework, it will show by the confidence you possess in the interview.

Categories of questions

Now, let's discuss the interview itself. People often ask me what questions I should expect in a job interview, and honestly, there is no tried-and-true list to make you completely ready for a cybersecurity interview. However, there is an approach I take to preparing for these questions. After years of being on both sides of the technical interview, I have learned that the questions fall into four areas:

- Your résumé
- The job description
- The required hard skills
- The necessary soft skills

Your résumé

The first group of questions you can expect in the job interview will be about your résumé. First, they will ask about previous employers and why you left each company. Next, they will ask about the education, experience, skills, and certifications you have listed in your résumé. Finally, be prepared for some in-depth questions where they may ask you to describe an instance where you used a specific skill. What is important to remember is that if you put it on your résumé, you must defend it. If something on your résumé proves to be false later, the company could use that to dismiss you, so be truthful.

The Job Description

As I stated in the previous chapter, the job description is your road map for the interview and the questions that the interviewer(s) will ask. Remember, the job description lists the required qualifications, skills, and experience for the position. You can expect questions focusing on how your knowledge, skills, and experience meet their requirements. Look at the job description, print it out, and then lay it next to your résumé and compare the two documents. I like to highlight areas in my résumé that meet the requirements in the job description document. I use this method to focus my preparations. You will never satisfy the complete list of expectations an employer is looking for in a position, so instead, focus on the 80% and how you are an exceptional candidate in those areas. If you can tell your value story of how you can meet at least 80% of their requirements, you should make it into the final round of interviews. It is good to write down these value stories and review them so that you are comfortable delivering them during your interview.

Required Hard Skills

This group may not just involve questions; it may require you to demonstrate a specific skill such as writing code in Python or changing an access control list on a firewall. When I was a security architect, it was not uncommon to have the interview divided into a panel interview and then transition to a lab or network room to demonstrate my skills and experience. This part of an interview is typically for higher-level technical positions. However, I mention this so you know that sometimes it's required, and it is becoming more common for entry-level positions.

Required Soft Skills

This final area is one that many people feel is the hardest. The interview tends to switch to scenario-based questions, and many times there are no right or wrong answers. When speaking to hiring managers about these questions, the focus will be on how you would handle a situation. Remember, this part of the conversation is about "fit" – will you be a good fit for the current team, the organization, its culture, or a specific program or job role. It is hard to prepare for scenario-based questions; you can do some research and find the basic ones most organizations ask you. Be honest, and don't be afraid to ask for clarification or for them to restate the question so you better understand what they are looking for in an answer.

Questions you can ask

By this time in the interview process, you have made it through their questions, and with a sigh of relief, you feel great because you think you are done. However, you're not done yet because interviews are a two-way process; don't forget that you get to ask questions. That's right; think of this as your turn to interview them to make sure the job and the company are a good fit for you. Let's look at some possible questions you can ask them. I will note why some of them are important. Remember, during the interview, take notes and especially write down whom you are speaking with, so when you ask them some of the following questions, you can ask them by their name. When you do this, it makes the discussion and the answers they provide you more personal.

What does a typical day in this job look like?

> I ask this to see if they understand the position and if the answers align with what I think I would be doing in the role. If I speak to multiple people over an interview process and each has different ideas, that could be a red flag about the position.

What are your company's values? What do you look for in employees to represent those values?

> The answer to this question will give you an idea of the soft skills, experience, personalities, and personal values they look for in candidates and what they will expect from you as an employee.

How would you describe the work environment here?

> Hopefully, the answer is a positive one. If the answer is too short or too pat, ask a follow-up question such as: "Can you say more?" You want to get an answer that seems authentic. That doesn't mean it has to balance good and bad, just that it appears to be their words and not corporate speak.

How does this position contribute to the organization/business unit/department/team's success?

This answer will give you an idea of how the job fits into the company. If it's a new role, they may not have an answer, and if it's entry-level, the answer may be pretty basic.

What do you hope I will accomplish in this position?

The answer to this question will give you some insight into what they expect of you. However, from personal experience, it usually is not in the job description, so pay attention.

What's your favorite part about working at the company?

This question is pretty standard, but I like to ask to see what they value about working at the company.

How do leaders encourage employees to ask questions?

I have always found the answer to this question interesting because it gives me insight into how I can ask for help if needed and whether the company encourages mentorship.

What does success look like in this position, and how do you measure it?

I highly recommend you ask this question. It will let you know how you will be evaluated and will give you valuable insight into how you are graded against peers, goals, or specific metrics.

Are employees involved in structuring their own goals and tasks?

The answer to this question will provide insight into whether your work and tasks will be micromanaged or you will have more freedom to grow and learn professionally in the position.

How often do you evaluate employee performance?

The two most common models are annual, as part of a corporate "pay for performance" review cycle, or annually on the anniversary of your hire. If the answer is that they handle raises, evaluations, and promotions on an "as-needed basis," you will want to dig deeper with follow-ups such as "How often are raises typically granted?" and "How do I qualify for a raise?" Vague answers can be a red flag that management might be arbitrary in evaluating, compensating, and promoting.

Are there opportunities for professional development? If so, what does that include?

The cybersecurity field is continually changing, so you want to see if they allow you to attend and pay for vendor training, security conferences, or certification training. Suppose the expectation is that you pay for them yourself. In that case, you need to factor this into your decision about the company being a good fit for you professionally or negotiate for more salary to pay for it out of pocket.

If the job is part of a team, ask for information about the team and its responsibilities.

The job description may be specific to the role, but you may find that your team has other responsibilities that were not listed. It's best to know that before accepting the position.

Ask the hiring manager, "What are some of the challenges of the job?"

This is another important question that will often give you clues about the non-technical aspects of the job. For example, are there budget constraints? Is a particular department challenging to work with? Are the company priorities blowing in the wind? Pay close attention to this answer.

Concluding the interview

As the interview ends, they have asked their questions, and you have done the same. Now it's time to finish the interview, and you guessed it – there are some questions you should ask.

Typically, multiple candidates will apply for a job, and you will not know if you are the candidate that gets the role. There are a couple of questions I usually ask to understand the next steps, and the answers provide a view into their process and if I have made it to the next round. The key questions:

What's the next step of this process, and when can I expect to hear from you?

> Usually, they will say they are still doing interviews with other candidates, and they will provide a point of contact who will reach out to you.

Is there anything about my experience or résumé that makes you question whether I am a good fit for this position?

> This question helps you collect feedback. I always ask this question to gauge how well I did with my interview preparations. Sometimes you will find that a specific skill or experience is the critical thing they are looking for, and don't be surprised if they didn't put it in the job description. So, chalk that up to experience and don't let it get you down. Just focus on preparing for your next interview.

After the interview, I recommend taking one last step while you are waiting for their answer about whether you got the job or not. Send your point of contact and interviewers a note to thank them for the opportunity to interview for the role. A thank you note leaves a good impression, and even if this job was not a fit, you might find yourself applying to that very same company in the future.

The Cybersecurity Interview ~ Chris

The key to a successful interview is to show the hiring manager how you can help solve potential business pain points (or problems) and how your skills and experience will enhance the capabilities of the current security team. For example, the only reasons a company hires someone are:

- there is too much work for the existing staff
- they need to backfill a recent departure
- they lack specific capabilities to complete their business mission

During research on the company or in the interview, try to find out which reasons apply to this job.

Ideally, finding this out from your recruiter will help you target your approach to the interview and tailor your responses to interviewers. For example, you will not highlight your specialty skills if the role fills a gap in workload. Instead, you would try to highlight your ability to make things more efficient, work well in teams, and improve processes. Conversely, if the hiring manager is looking for a specialist, not highlighting how you meet those needs will be detrimental to your interview outcome. Below I will describe some of the ways to prepare for the interview in the best way possible.

Research the role

By researching the role, you can determine whether that role focuses on specific processes or generalized workload management. Sometimes, the cues for this can come from the job description, feedback, and reviews on job portals, or informational interviews conducted on the role. For example, some Security Operation Center (SOC) analyst roles focus on volume at the lower level by concentrating on how many alerts they can address within an hour or a day. However, higher-tier SOC analyst roles are focused on analysis and managing complex problems, finding trends, and discovering a mitigation strategy for the organization.

A case in point: I have often stopped interviews early if the role as described, the manager, or the recruiter requires something that I don't want to do, or the company's culture feels off. I have approached it with two mindsets: continue the interview to practice my delivery, fully knowing that I am not interested in the role; or stop cold, state that I am not interested in the position for these reasons and terminate it. Some reasons that I have ended an interview instantly included unethical approaches, undesirable culture, and requirements or job duties that are a critical part of the role which I know I don't want to do. So, you might ask, why might I have applied for a position if there were job duties that I didn't want to do? I have noticed that the job description does not always match the role. There is often some disconnect in the hiring process when it comes to the actual job compared to the job description. So even if you don't meet all the listed requirements, consider accepting the interview if you are invited; you can always end it early if you find out that it is not a fit.

Research the company

While some roles across companies may be similar regardless of whether they are focused on volume or quality, that is generally not the case and will vary from company to company. Therefore, finding out the focus of the position within a company is essential. You can address this by doing informational interviews with peers before the interview process. If you cannot do this, sometimes you can find out this information from company blogs, job portal reviews, or public interviews, which company leaders might have done. Researching the company and discovering new lines of business can also hint at what they might need. For example, suppose they signed a significant contract with the government or a company to partner or deliver on a particular service. The nature of these services can provide insight into what new capabilities they might need for the open role.

Hopefully, you have already researched the company by this stage in the process to ensure that you align with their business objectives. At the least, ensure that their mission aligns with your values and beliefs. These elements and a few others, like management style, and levels of collaboration, constitute a company's culture. Suppose the company culture diverges significantly from your preferred culture. In that case, it will eventually become a divider in your relationship with the company and could cause you to resent your role there. Based on my experience, working for a company that has a culture you disagree with will eventually drive you to be frustrated with decisions made, your daily workload, and ultimately, lead to burnout. Burnout is incredibly real if you become frustrated because of these differences. Life is too short to work in a burnout factory, so do your research on the company.

Research the interviewer

If possible, try to get information from the job post or the recruiter as to who the interviewer will be so that you can research their background. For example, you'll want to know if they live and work locally, how long they have been with the company, the evolution of their career, or any particular views on their role or their passions which they might have posted on social media. Having some of this personal information will allow you to build a mutual connection with your interviewer. While most interviewers will try to be equal to all applicants, subconsciously, they might form a connection with someone with shared interests. Even interviewers looking for diverse candidates from various backgrounds and perspectives may still have this affinity. It's a deep part of the human psyche. Note that there is no value to being insincere or faking a shared interest. But showing an interest or sharing where you do have things in common can be a great way to form a connection.

Now that you have a great understanding of the role, the company, and the interviewer, it is time to show how you are best suited for the position and bring the most value to the organization. One of the goals of the interviewers is to find out if the candidate can complete the tasks required for the position, solve any specific business problems, and fit in with the company culture and the team.

Your goal is to demonstrate that you have the skills, competencies, and experience that are essential for being successful in the role and that you are a fit for what they need. One of the easiest ways to do this is through storytelling. Practicing this storytelling ahead of time will allow you to share your experience with the interviewer effectively. To do this, first you have to think about stories that best demonstrate your ability to analyze a business situation, tackle complications, and solve complex problems. Then it would be best if you practiced this by working with someone to simulate an interview and adjust based on their feedback. Another option, if you don't have someone who can objectively help you in this process, is to look in a mirror or record yourself and tweak your responses based on observed mistakes.

There are several ways to construct a story for concisely communicating what the interviewer might be looking for in a candidate.

STAR Method

The Situation, Task, Action, and Results method is one popular way of sharing these stories. This method allows the interviewer to understand what was happening at the time, what you determined was the task that needed to be done to resolve the problem, what specific actions you took, and what results those actions yielded. You must describe precisely what you did in these situations. Based on my experience, candidates often focus on how their team approached, tackled, and resolved the problem, but that does not help the interviewer to understand what your role was in this process.

You can mention what the team did, but it is critical that you dissect these situations and highlight your specific role in the case.

Based on the informational interviews or the analysis of the job description, you should determine what you think are the three or four most critical skills or competencies required for the role and develop STAR stories based on those areas of focus. Remember, your role in these stories is vital, and what the interviewers need to evaluate your performance or potential performance based on your past actions.

Behavioral Interviews

Behavioral interviews focus on what you have done in the past with the idea that they will be a predictor of future performance. In this form of interviewing, the interviewer will ask specific questions about what you did within a particular situation, what actions you took, and what the results were. This method might seem similar to the STAR method because it is, except the interviewer asks you a particular question and monitors your response vs. you creating the narrative.

Don't let the fact that the interviewer is asking these specific questions throw you off. By preparing ahead of time, you can respond to these questions easily. As with the STAR method, if you can think of stories that would address the core behaviors or actions that would make you successful in a role, you can prepare and practice these stories ahead of time.

Situation / Complication / Resolution

The last method of storytelling you might use to effectively convey that you have the skills, competencies, and behaviors needed to be successful in a role is the situation, complication, resolution structure. This structure might be most useful for analysis-driven work but can still be used for all functions. In this form of storytelling, similar to the STAR method, you start by setting up the situation for the interviewer, including elements like the role, the industry, and the specific challenge. Then you pivot to the complication. The complication is where you redirect to the business problem and the impact it is having on the business. This part is critical; by sharing the impact, you show your ability to dissect the problem and determine its holistic effect on the business. The resolution focuses both on what you did to help mitigate the impact and any recommendations you had for future improvements or how to prevent similar problems from happening in the future. Do not just stop at solving the problem. Take the last step of analyzing the root cause and making performance improvements for the future.

Storytelling is an essential interview technique that allows you to effectively convey your actions and the impact on the organization to the interviewer to show the value that you can bring to their company. Use this time to show your personality and passion for the subject and see the responses from the interviewer. You won't have to look too hard for the opportunity to share your stories. One easy trigger would be a question that starts with "Tell me about a time when…" or something similar. That's an indicator that the interviewer is actually looking for you to share a story. But be prepared to jump to a story based on other openings such as "What was a key achievement at company Z?" or "What was the biggest problem you had to overcome?" or "What are you most proud of?" These are openings that you can use to show how you would help the company solve its problems.

Interviewing the interviewer

Interviews are a two-way street, and so far, we have focused on the company asking you questions, but you should also be interviewing the company.

Whether the interviewer is a recruiter, peer, or hiring manager, you can glean information about the company culture, mission, vision, and values from them. You want to ensure that the company operates in a manner that aligns with your values, or you will likely not be happy there and burn out. Asking questions is your time to find out whether they like working there, whether you would enjoy working with them, and what it is like there or what a day is like working in this position.

Here are some examples of questions you might use:

1. Stepping into my shoes, would you interview for this company again? Why?
2. What are some of the challenges and rewards of working for this company?
3. What might you change about the company culture or environment? Why?

Being sure to tailor and prepare these questions ahead of time will allow you both to ensure that the company meets your requirements of what you are looking for in a company, role, team, or manager, and show the interviewers that you have thoughtfully prepared for the interview.

Finding a role in which you will be both happy and prosperous is about ensuring the company, team, and role align with your values and that the position will sufficiently challenge you in growing your skills and competencies. Therefore, you should ensure that these interviews are both about finding the right company and role for you, as well as showing the company how they would benefit from hiring you to be on their team.

The Job Interview ~ Renee

Congratulations! You've made it to the cyber interview! You did everything right – including gaining cyber experience, education, and maybe a certification. Your résumé and profile piqued the interest of a recruiter or hiring manager and you are a few steps away from a potential job offer. There are multiple components to the interview and your expectations should be set for what the interview process entails. I will share information from the perspective of a recruiter with additional insights from receiving feedback from the hiring team.

When you are invited to the first interview, this is an opportunity for a quick introduction so the hiring team can learn more about you and you can learn more about the company. These initial screening calls are typically less than 30 minutes and almost always via phone or Zoom. Your primary goal should be to show your enthusiasm and passion for security. It's also a time to showcase your skills and answer any questions the leaders may have about your experience. During this initial screen, the recruiter or hiring leader is trying to assess if you have the skills that align to the position. They will ask you to tell them about yourself and will ask questions to determine if you are either a fit for that specific role or a fit for the organization. Take every opportunity to learn as much as you can about the team, the organization, and the projects.

Preparation

As you prepare for your interview, there are many things to research to be fully prepared for the conversation. You will want to research the company, the interviewers, the team, and any projects they are working on.

First on the list is to research the company to see if there has been any recent news. Also, go to their website's career page and their LinkedIn career page to hear directly from them on what they view as important aspects of being a part of their team. For example, do they pride themselves on being a flat, nimble organization? Do the pictures of the staff look more laid back, or is it a formal, corporate environment? This gives you a glimpse into the culture of the organization and what they deem as important. You will want to echo some of the sentiments of the site that pique your interest in the interview. Another place to get feedback on companies is Glassdoor. Research the company reviews and reviews from people who are in the job for which you're interviewing. Get a feel for the organization through the employee comments. This is also a great place to learn about compensation ranges for companies.

Next, research the people who are interviewing you. Review their LinkedIn pages and search for any presentations on YouTube or articles they may have published. Make a note of their professional experience and their interests. Look at their longevity at the company and see if they have grown in responsibility during their time there. Have they given talks? Review prior presentations so you get a glimpse of who you'll be meeting for your interview. The more research you do, the more you will be armed with a variety of information to make you confident in the interview. If you'd like to dig deep, you can reach out to someone on LinkedIn who works in the department where you're interviewing. You'd be surprised at how eager some people are to discuss their projects and share insights about the team.

You will also want to learn about the team's current technology stack and projects that are on the horizon. Have you worked with the technologies before? Is there a technology there that you are eager to learn? A few internet searches looking at previous job openings will give you an idea of the technologies they currently use. This information can help you prepare for technical questions they may ask in the interview.

As you research, prepare a list of questions that you want answers to. These could be related to the company culture, projects, tech stack, or anything else that interests you. Then, armed with information about the company, the individuals, and thoughtful questions, you will be well prepared to participate in the interview.

The Interview Process

The interview process can range from an extremely fast process with as little as one phone interview to multiple interviews with candidates flying to onsite interviews. It could take weeks or months before the company decides. It all depends on the company and the number of interviews conducted. You should ask what the interview process is going to be like during the first call. This knowledge helps in a few ways – it helps to set your expectations for the interviews and how long the process will take, and it helps you navigate multiple interviews and offer timelines.

Recruiter screening questions

When a recruiter reaches out for the initial phone screen (aka the first interview), they are trying to confirm that the experience that they noticed in your LinkedIn profile or résumé aligns with the job description that they are working on. They will ask about your current and recent experience and will want you to elaborate on your current situation and projects. Although there are typically multiple interviews, beginning with a recruiter interview/screen, a technical interview, and possibly additional interviews, the first one is important as the recruiter is often the primary gatekeeper for the hiring manager.

More often than not, the recruiter screening interview is to rule you in or out based on the hiring manager's criteria. In addition to basic questions like, "Why are you looking for a new opportunity?" and "Why our company?" some managers will provide a few screening questions to determine if a person could be a fit for the role. These questions range from specific technical questions to more general questions about a person's work history. From a technical perspective, a manager will want to know the depth of a person's expertise, and the recruiter will ask that a person rate themselves on their technical depth in a specific skill. A short technical review with a tool like HackerRank or CodeLive is often a part of the screening interview. For example, if the manager asks for deep expertise in Python and you rate yourself as a 5 out of 10, you are likely not the right fit for that role. If you participate in the technical review and you can't complete the assignment, that could also be a reason to rule you out.

A request that often comes up from managers from a work history perspective is that the person stayed long enough to impact or complete the project. Managers realize that people may not last at one place for a long time; however, they want to hear that you completed the projects assigned to you. If you have a new job every few months and this manager is seeking someone with longevity, this will be a red flag for them. On the other hand, some managers are okay with having people who have worked on multiple short-term contracts. It really is case by case.

A case in point: I recently screened a potential candidate for a senior cybersecurity engineer position. The manager wanted a full-time employee who would drive a project to completion and estimated it would take 14 months. The person I was screening had multiple Fortune 100 roles on his LinkedIn profile that were shorter-term (meaning less than a year). Because of the short duration of the jobs, I assumed they were contracts, but he told me that these were full-time positions. I asked him why he was entertaining new opportunities, and he shared that he was always keeping his options open. This hired-gun approach was a red flag for me for this role. I shared the information with the manager, who also wanted to know why this person was job-hopping and wondered if this person couldn't handle the roles that they take on.

Red flags also come up when there are unexplained gaps in employment. Again, the key word is "unexplained." Managers will want to know why a person took time off. If there was a family situation, then share that. If you decided to take an extended vacation in between assignments or went to school full-time, that's fine too. You don't have to go into detail but let the recruiter or manager know why you weren't working.

The most crucial aspect of nailing the screening interview – and all interviews – is to know yourself. Know your strengths and weaknesses. Be honest about what you can and cannot do. Know when it sounds like the opportunity is the right fit or not. This self-awareness may sound cliché, but you will likely get a sense of whether the role (or company) sounds like the right fit for you and be able to articulate that.

Another case in point: I recently screened someone for a senior cybersecurity analyst role. She immediately asked me if the position was an engineer and shared that she was more of an administrator. She was forthright in her answers about what she did and didn't know. Even though she didn't have the right experience, she said she was eager to learn. I liked her personality and thought she could be a fit for a junior position at my client. When the hiring manager screened her, he also thought she would be a good fit for the team and commented on how aware she was of her strengths and weaknesses. Unlike many others, she didn't try to fake it. She was clear on what she could and couldn't do, which was impressive to the hiring manager and me.

The next most important aspect of navigating the screening interview is to do some research on the company. You'd be surprised at the number of people that I've screened that know zero about the company. A 20-minute Google search on the latest company news and a look at their Careers page is all you need. So many people don't even do that.

As shared above, there are hiring manager interviews after the recruiter interviews. They will provide the recruiter with feedback after their interviews. The positive feedback I have heard most as a recruiter is that the candidate has the skills that align with what they are seeking, and the candidate is passionate about security. Those are the top things to keep in mind and demonstrate when interviewing. Often, the company will decline to move forward with a candidate if they do not have the technical skills needed to do the job. There are many other reasons a company may decline to move forward that often have nothing to do with the individual. The takeaway here is to gain as much experience as you can and show how passionate you are about it, so be prepared.

Chapter 9 – Key Points and Recommended Actions

- Interviewing for every job is different. The process can range from a single phone interview to multiple interviews over several weeks. Work with the recruiter to understand the process so you can fully prepare and avoid surprises.
- Interviewing begins with research. Use the research techniques you learned in Chapter 8 along with the human network you built in Chapters 6 and 7 to research the position, company, and interviewer(s).
- Analyze the job description to determine the questions you'll be asked and line your résumé up to the description to know how you'll tie your experience and capabilities to job requirements.
- Prepare and practice stories so you are ready to answer the soft-skill interview questions you are likely to encounter.
- Review the questions that we have suggested you consider to get a clear picture of the position you are considering and whether or not it's a good fit for you.
- Remember to show your passion for the domain. More than most, cybersecurity is a mission-driven industry. After the work you did in Chapter 1 to determine if this is the right field for you, let that come through.

Chapter 10

Recruiters and How to Use Them in Your Job Search

Introduction

As you develop a career plan for how you will get into the cybersecurity field, make sure you have room in the plan to meet and work with recruiters. The purpose of this chapter is to explain the different types of recruiters you might encounter and how they fit into the process of generating the candidate pool for any given job opening.

We use the term "recruiter" as a catchall for an entire field. As you'll see in the essays that follow, it's critical to know the role and motivations of the person you are working with when trying to land an interview with a hiring manager.

Larger companies that think in terms of a talent lifecycle have internal processes for uncovering, recruiting, and developing the people who become the company's lifeblood. They expend as much energy on cultural fit as they do on skillset and salary matching. Regardless of the organization's size, there is often a mix of internal and external resources they turn to when looking for the next perfect hire.

As you read each essay, you'll see recruiters described from slightly different angles. But, putting all three together, you'll come away with a complete understanding of the people who are the gatekeepers, or gateways, to your dream job.

Working with Recruiters in Cybersecurity – Some Basics You Should Know ~ Gary

You have decided to pursue a career in cybersecurity, but you have also realized that many of the jobs you would like to apply for require you to speak with a recruiter. While every field has its share of recruiters, right now there are many of them in cybersecurity due to the current need for talent. Unfortunately, not all of these recruiters understand our industry. This chapter will cover the basics you need to be aware of when working with recruiters; they will help you tune your job search process and provide you with a reference to use throughout your career.

To begin, let's cover a few basic facts about recruiters.

Recruiters work for the companies that hire them

Never forget that recruiters don't work for you because you are not paying their fees and commissions. They must present viable candidates to the companies that have hired them. If they tell you that you're not a fit for a job, you probably aren't a fit. There were several times that I wanted to argue with a recruiter because I just knew that I would be a fantastic candidate for a particular position. But my recruiter said, "no." In retrospect, I realize the recruiter knew I wouldn't fit into that organization's culture or knew the hiring manager wanted specific skills or experience that I lacked. Recruiters get paid to bring candidates that could be a fit. If they tell you that you aren't, don't take it personally; just ask to look at another role.

Recruiters want to find someone for the job

Recruiters from staffing agencies that have been hired by companies to help them fill their positions are typically paid on commission. In many cases, if they don't provide the successful candidate, they don't get paid. This creates a powerful incentive to fill the job. But with that in mind, this process should be a two-way relationship. This is a "people" business, and good recruiters genuinely want to help. Recruiters who are invested in good outcomes for both parties are interested in brokering the right deal. Certainly, tell them what your requirements are, but listen to what they say. They will often know the "real" salary range. And they have usually seen many candidates, so they can also help you gauge what you can likely command for a salary.

That said, if you think you are being coerced into accepting an offer that is too low, remember that you control the situation; just say no. There is no reason to take a job unless it's right for you and you feel good about the decision. But listen to the recruiter. If they tell you that there is a pay band and what you are asking for is way outside what the company is willing to pay for this role, see if there are other possibilities to get what you need. Consider options such as a hiring bonus, annual bonus, or equity. It doesn't hurt to ask. Get creative.

Recruiters don't know everything

Unless the hiring company employs the recruiter, don't be surprised if they don't always know everything about a particular job. This problem is especially true for technical roles. I research the company, the hiring manager, team members, previous open positions, and, when possible, speak to prior employees. This effort will provide you with some context on the role and the hiring company. If you are working with a third-party recruiter, the only information they have is what the company provides them. Do your research so you can fill in the gaps of what the recruiter might not know.

Now that we have reviewed basic facts about working with recruiters, I want to discuss the characteristics of good recruiters and cover what recruiters don't provide to you as a candidate. First, I believe it is crucial to understand that working with a recruiter in a job search shouldn't be a distasteful process. Some recruiters that I have worked with have become close friends over the years, as I appreciate the service they provide to our community. However, I never forget they work for the company that pays their commission. One last note, anyone can call themselves a recruiter without knowing much about the jobs they're recruiting for, so do your homework. Remember, research not just the role and company you are interested in but the recruiter you will work with because doing this work will pay dividends in not wasting your time during a job search.

At a minimum, good recruiters should be communicative and truthful with you at so that you both aren't wasting time. Good recruiters can also help you in several ways, including:

Good recruiters should tell your story

What I mean by that is they should understand more about you than just your résumé. They should have spent time with you to understand your history, what's important to you, your career goals, and your personality. This knowledge and understanding will honestly help you in the long run. The recruiter can now present you as a whole package to the hiring company or screen you from interviewing at companies that are not a good fit for your personality and career goals.

Good recruiters can provide insight into a role

Remember that the recruiter has been hired to fill a particular position, know what the hiring manager and company are looking for, and what the candidates' level of experience and skills should be for the job. The recruiter can give you feedback on how you stack up against your competition and should be able to provide some ideas on changes you might want to make to your résumé to best represent the skills and experience you have to offer the prospective employer.

Good recruiters will notify you of hidden opportunities

A good recruiter will typically have an extensive network of peers and employers they have served. They will know about opportunities that are confidential and hopefully a good fit for you. Recruiters that I have worked with over the years have checked in with me to see if I was interested in an opportunity or if I knew someone they could speak to about filling a new role. If you find a good recruiter, establish a relationship. They may not have something for you today, but tomorrow can be a new opportunity.

Good recruiters will have experience in helping you prepare

With the experience a good recruiter has in the industry, they can advise salary ranges for specific opportunities. They can also provide feedback on your expectations and help you prepare for your interview. For instance, they might tell you what the hiring manager might focus on, that might not be obvious from the job description.

Now, as we have this vision of a good recruiter in our minds, let's discuss what recruiters don't provide.

They are not representing just you

There is a good chance that the recruiter you are working with has several candidates they are submitting for the role you want. Don't take it personally; remember that the company hires them to find candidates, and therefore you should be working with multiple recruiters. The more opportunities you work, the more chances you will find the security team that is waiting for you. So, get to work.

It's not personal

The recruiter you are working with is the one advocating for you in the hiring process. However, they don't decide who moves forward or not in the process, so don't get upset with them if they tell you the company is passing on you; it's nothing personal. If you can get feedback from your recruiter, ask for it; sometimes, they may have gleaned some information on how the interviews are going, and that knowledge can help better prepare you for your next opportunity.

The recruiter isn't a career coach

They might help you get ready for your interview and possibly even assist with negotiation preparations. But remember, they are recruiters hired by a firm to fill their open positions; don't lose sight of that when working with them. Sometimes recruiters who have been in the field for a long time might spot gaps in your experience and offer sound advice. But remember, they are only a recruiter, they are not working in the job. As I have stated before, do your homework, talk to your network, and come prepared.

Your recruiter doesn't always have a position for you

So don't think they are ignoring you, even though it may feel that way. Recruiters tend to work open roles in batches, and sometimes they have jobs they think you would be a fit for, and sometimes they don't. Just as they submit multiple candidates for a role, you should work with several recruiters. Remember, the more opportunities you work, the more chances you have of finding your next position.

I hope, from the points I have covered in this chapter, that you now have a better understanding of how to work with recruiters when you search for a job. Recruiters are a fantastic resource to help you understand an industry or a role that you want. However, they are not the only method for finding a job. Don't forget you have a network of peers, professional organizations, mentors, and friends that can help you as well. So, employ all your resources as part of your next job search strategy, and I sincerely hope you find the position that is right for you.

How Best to Use a Recruiter ~ Chris

Many people looking for new jobs come across recruiters, sourcers, and headhunters, but they don't always understand what these people do. Each has a specific role in the recruitment cycle. Although it might vary by company, these are general descriptions of the functions and the services that they perform.

- Sourcer – Sourcers typically use job boards, social media sites, schools, and other tools to look for potential candidates who might be a good fit for the open roles they are looking to fill. In larger companies, they might also do an introductory call to test your interest in a position before advancing you in the process. When Small-Medium-Businesses (SMBs) use sourcers, they are typically only responsible for collecting and inputting résumés into the applicant tracking systems. Sourcers are generally entry-level positions in the recruiting industry.

- Recruiter – Depending on the company's size, a recruiter could handle anything from finding the candidates up to and including onboarding new hires. They usually have a solid understanding of the company's needs, often down to the group level. They are often responsible for building a pipeline of candidates as well as proactively looking for potential recruits. They sometimes help with offer negotiation as well. Sometimes recruiters focus on particular roles or groups, but they could handle openings across the company.

- Headhunter – Similar to recruiters looking for candidates to fill roles, they typically specialize in filling specific types of roles or industries. For example, some headhunters specialize in filling CISO and senior IT security leadership roles specifically for IT-focused startups.

- Agencies – Temporary staffing agencies/ staffing agencies are companies that help organizations with their needs to find ideal candidates to fill roles. Some of these companies specialize in specific industries and generally provide better results because they understand the industry better, while those that generalize usually focus on sourcing pools of candidates with less emphasis on the individual candidates' quality.

To work with these people most effectively in your search, you need to know when and where to use them. It is also critical to understand that these recruiters work for the companies looking to hire (their clients) and not the candidates searching for roles. While some of these recruiters have the best intentions and try to help the candidates as much as possible, they might only have access to a small subset of roles for a company or industry. For most individual contributor candidates, if they don't have an active job search that they think you qualify for, they won't be in a position to help you.

This dynamic means that candidates are likely to end up working with many recruiters throughout their job search. The only word of caution comes when working with multiple sourcers, recruiters, and headhunters working at different agencies. You want to make sure that you know the roles they are submitting you for and that you do not work with multiple agencies looking to fill the same position. The last thing you want is to have several agencies submitting you to the same company for the same role because you don't want to give the impression you've sprayed your résumé all over town looking for the first job you can get. You want to make the company feel like you want to work for them.

Getting the inside scoop!

Sometimes the best insight into a potential company comes from their internal recruiters. Outside resources like agencies might not know the key differentiators for a particular role or even why you might want to work for the company. If you are lucky enough to be talking to an internal or in-house recruiter, use this conversation to discover more information about the company. Ask about their culture and how they measure performance. Try to find out how urgently they are trying to fill this position and whether this a new position or a backfill for someone who left. If it is a backfill, find out why the position is vacant. Was it a promotion (a hopeful sign), or did the person leave (ask why)? Feel free to ask these types of questions, and trust your gut feeling when you hear the answers. Sometimes it might be a dream company on paper, but once you start to find out more about it, it might not be so dreamy after all. The recruiter will try to qualify you for the role and use the conversation to qualify the company and position against your criteria.

Putting your best foot forward

It is easy to overlook the pivotal role that recruiters play in the initial screening process. Usually, they are the ones who decide whether the hiring manager reviews your résumé. Thus, presenting candidates to the hiring manager is where the distinction between external and internal recruiters becomes evident.

External recruiters are likely to be the first gate in the process. While you need to impress them to move on, they often operate on the volume of candidates that they can submit to an organization. Thus, their job is often to create a pool of candidates.

Internal recruiters are the next gate; they validate that you meet the requirements and might rank you against the other candidates in the pool. Internal recruiters are more focused on the cultural fit, providing hiring managers with a shortlist of candidates and scheduling interviews.

Both types of recruiters can make the go or no-go decision, so you want to treat them with the same respect as the hiring manager. As a hiring manager, the feedback from recruiters has often influenced my decision to set up an interview with a potential candidate. While the ultimate hack of the process is to bypass them and get straight to the hiring manager, that is not always possible.

When to follow up?

Being in good communication with the recruiter will allow you to keep in touch with the progress of and find ways to get feedback on the process. Typically, if expectations are not set for the next steps, following up with them once a week is an excellent cadence. On the other hand, they might be filling various roles and scheduling different people. Therefore, they might not get you a daily update on the progress.

It's a give and take relationship built over the long run

Recruiters typically work for multiple companies or agencies throughout their careers. If you find one that understands you and your desired path, try to develop a trust-based relationship for the long run. You never know when they might have that next role in your career path. This long-term relationship should also be a two-way street. Help them with referrals to your connections if you have someone in mind for a role they are looking to fill. Not only will this build stronger bonds with the individuals that you are referring to for jobs, but it creates a mutual connection with a great recruiter.

I have built many relationships with recruiters and have known many of them for years. Recruiters can also be great sounding boards for the job market and help you with conversations about promotions or position changes, even within your own company. They can share the current market conditions for those, providing you with the best bargaining position with your leadership. Using insights from recruiters like the current market pay scale for a role in a particular area or industry can ensure that you get the best possible offer. In addition, they could help you increase the hiring company's offer package outside of salary, which you might not have considered. During my career, sometimes I overlooked things like vacation days, sign-on bonuses, or even additional training dollars during my offer negotiation and was reminded by my recruiter connections to consider these benefits.

The Recruiter's Role ~ Renee

"Recruiters and managers need to stop creating unrealistic job descriptions so we can apply and not get rejected," says one LinkedIn user.

"HR and recruiters don't give us a chance to get through and share our experience with the hiring manager. Although I don't have the exact experience, I have certifications and the right skills and I get no response," says another.

On any given day on LinkedIn, there is a plethora of comments blaming HR and recruiters for the hiring process. Some of that blame is definitely warranted, but most of it is not. Many early-career individuals are unaware that recruiters are usually not the one writing the job description. That role is squarely on the hiring manager, with minor edits from HR and recruiters. There is no way for a recruiter to know the intricate details of what is needed for a cybersecurity role. Just as it would be unrealistic for a recruiter to write a job description for a pilot, a chef, or a physician, it is unrealistic for a recruiter to write a job description for a cybersecurity role.

A recruiter's job is to fill open positions. Recruiters are candidates' biggest cheerleaders as they want candidates who are a fit for the role to get the opportunity to interview for the position. Job seekers think recruiters are against them when in reality, we want them to get the job. It's in a recruiter's best interest to get the best person for the job in front of the hiring manager.

There tend to be misunderstandings about the recruiter's role in the hiring process, so I will explain the most common types of recruiters in companies and their role in getting people hired. For many of you current working in large organizations, this will be information you already know. However, for newbies, this will help you understand how recruiting works.

First, there are a few things that I want to highlight when it comes to recruiting. **External Recruiters** work for and are paid by the company that hired them to find candidates with a specific skill set that they cannot find on their own. The recruiter's allegiance is to that company. Some external recruiters have salaries, but many are paid only by commission. **Internal Recruiters and Sourcers** are also tasked with finding specific types of talent for the hiring manager's needs. They are often stretched thin, with many hiring managers as their internal clients.

Internal company recruiting

Internal company recruiters work directly for the company making the hire. They typically are a part of the HR division but occasionally can be a part of the business or operations. For example, in large corporations, a recruiting department is usually part of HR. Along with Recruiting, also known as Talent Acquisition or The People Team, the other departments that make up HR are usually Payroll, Training & Development, Employee Relations, Compensation, Health & Wellness, and HR Business Partners.

Within the recruiting department, there is a typical chain of command. Depending on how large the company is, there can be a Recruiting VP, Recruiting Director, Recruiting Manager, Executive Recruiting, Recruiters, Sourcers, Campus Recruitment Team, Immigration lead, and recruiting assistants/schedulers. Smaller companies can have as few as one person performing all of these functions. One minute they can be handling someone's question about maternity leave and the next, recruiting cybersecurity professionals.

These are three sample org charts for different-sized organizations.

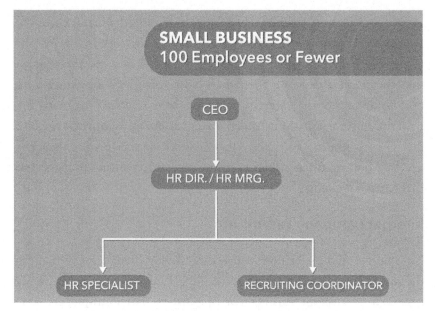

Figure 10.1 Small Business HR Department

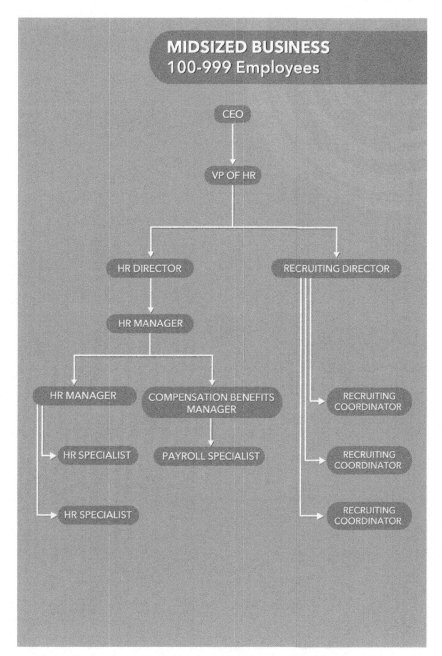

Figure 10.2 Midsized Business HR Department

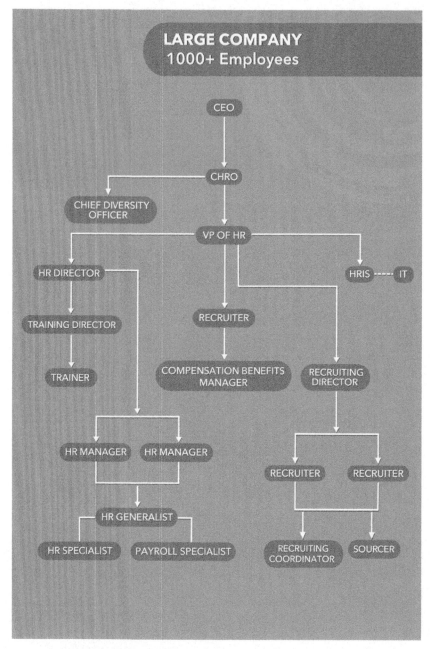

Figure 10.3 Large Company HR Department

External recruiters

External recruiters are recruiting companies that do not work for the company making the hire. Instead, they are a separate company that the organization engages to help fill their various positions. It is common to refer to these companies as Headhunters, Staffing Agencies, Temp Agencies, Recruitment Agencies, Search Firms, and Executive Recruiting Companies.

Their organizational structure is a bit different. The larger organizations like Robert Half have a Head of Business Operations, Account Managers, Recruiters, Payroll, and more. Smaller shops can have as few as a one or two people running the whole show. Some companies are very niche and only focus on a specific industry or type of roles. Other companies are broad and can recruit many different types of roles in a variety of industries. These companies have multiple clients. They might recruit a security analyst at PayPal, a security manager at Sony, and a dozen front-end software engineers at eBay all at the same time.

Someone breaking into cybersecurity who is working with recruiters from internal organizations will most likely interact with Recruiters, Campus or University Recruiters, Veteran/Military Recruiters, HR managers, Sourcers, or Sourcing Recruiters.

If you are working with external recruitment or staffing agencies, you will interact with recruiters.

Let's quickly define the different types of recruiting staff.

Internal company

- Recruiters – They are usually assigned a group of internal clients. The larger organizations will have recruiters dedicated to one part of the company. For example, they could be assigned to the Cybersecurity department or the Engineering department. On average a recruiter has 20 positions that they are working to fill, which can include up to the same number of hiring managers. Recruiters who partner with both hiring managers and candidates are also called "full lifecycle recruiters."

- Campus or University Recruiters – They perform exactly like the recruiter except that they focus on hiring interns and entry-level, college grads. They are typically assigned a target school list and make their hires from that list of schools.

- Veteran/Military Recruiters – They perform exactly like the recruiter except that they focus on hiring veterans. They can translate the military experience into corporate experience and shepherd veterans through the hiring process.

- HR Managers – Recruiting is just one component of their job. They could be juggling dealing with performance issues from an employee, someone taking leave for medical reasons, and recruiting a security architect.

- Sourcers or Sourcing Recruiters – Sourcers or Sourcing Recruiters are assigned a group of job descriptions to "source" or hunt talent. Sourcing is required typically for roles that don't get many applicants or may get many unqualified applicants. Sourcers usually do not interact often with the hiring manager. They are the "candidate-facing" person who does outreach to the candidates and then provides these vetted candidates to the recruiter, who will then pass them on to the hiring manager.

External company

External recruiters are either solely candidate-facing sourcers with limited interaction with the hiring manager or full lifecycle and work with both the manager and the candidates.

How to partner with recruiters

If you are a student at a university or a technical boot camp, connect with your university's career services department. They have partnerships with organizations that will be seeking interns and entry-level talent. If you're in a graduate program, many universities will provide resources for placing their graduate students as well. Universities' career services centers have career fairs and other resources to help their students find internship opportunities and jobs. In addition, career services also provide résumé-writing and interviewing skills courses for students.

Unless it's a staffing agency, external recruiters are seldom hired to find entry-level candidates for companies. Companies can go directly to a university or boot camp and hire the talent themselves versus spending their budget on searching for university graduates. The best use of an entry-level candidate's time is to network with internal company recruiters or directly with the company's leaders.

If you are transitioning from the same career but just switching industries, then external recruiters will be able to help you. In your case, you have directly transferable skills, and the external recruiter can tell you if you need to make any tweaks to your résumé to be in the best position to land an opportunity. An example is if you're in a marketing or sales role in a finance company and want to move into a similar role in a cybersecurity company.

If you are transitioning into security without the exact skills needed, an external recruiter is likely not going to be able to help place you into an opportunity. The companies hiring the external recruitment firm are hiring them to find specific people with skill sets that the company cannot find on their own. These are usually people already doing the job at another company. An example is if a leader at Bank of America is looking for a security architect with cloud experience. If the leader cannot find a person through Bank of America's recruitment team, they will hire an external recruitment firm that specializes in helping them find other security architects in financial services institutions. So, if you are a systems administrator and you're transitioning to a security architect, an external recruiter would not be able to help you in finding a new role.

People tend to overlook working with recruiters within their current company. If you can meet with the internal recruiters in your organization and explain that you are making a transition, they will be able to provide you with a wealth of knowledge regarding what the hiring manager is seeking when looking for someone to fill their role. Also, don't overlook speaking directly with the hiring managers to find out what would make you an attractive candidate for a role in their cybersecurity department.

The reason I have highlighted the roles and responsibilities of various recruiters is, so you know where to dedicate your time in the job search. Recruiters are a great resource, in some cases, but a better use of time is often connecting directly with your future leaders and peers in security.

Chapter 10 – Key Points and Recommended Actions

- The word "recruiter" carries a lot of freight. When you are working with someone in that broad category, find out what role they play as early as you can. Knowing this will save time and frustration.
- Just as interviews are two-way streets, so is the information exchange with recruiters. While they might be asking you about your experience, you should be asking them about the culture. If they ask you why you left your last role, you follow that up by asking why this role is open. It's not an interrogation – the goal is to build a rapport.
- Realize that recruiters are specialists in the art of recruiting but often generalists in the job roles they recruit. Internal recruiters especially will typically know a lot about the company's process and the overall culture. But they may struggle to answer what you might consider basic questions about technology. Keep this in mind when asking and answering questions. Don't give them a lot of technical nuances when answering questions about your experience.
- Relationships with recruiters can be quite beneficial over the long term. Just remember that if they don't have a role open that you might qualify for, they may not always have the time to be responsive. Don't take it personally.
- Your relationship with recruiters is a two-way street. They broker people. Their stock in trade is being able to bring roles to people and people to roles. So, help them if you can by recommending people you think would be good for a role they are trying to fill. But don't be indiscriminate, and never recommend someone for a role before checking with that person first.

Section 5

The Next Stage of Your Journey

Chapter 11

Working in Cybersecurity

Introduction

Getting your first job in cybersecurity is not the finish line, it's the starting line. In this chapter, we will discuss some strategies for staying at the top of your game and preparing you for a successful career in the cybersecurity industry.

That all starts with assessing where you are now and where you want to go. You might have performed a similar analysis in an earlier chapter, but by now you have a lot more insights into your new role and all that you have yet to learn.

Map out your career and what you might need to do to get there. Continuous education and certifications are some of the ways that many cybersecurity professionals continue to advance their careers. It provides them with new challenges, and they learn new things and stay up with the evolving industry.

Another way of ensuring that you are at the top of your game is to get a more experienced professional to help you through professional mentorship. Mentors can help you shortcut failures by learning from their mistakes as well as getting past unforeseen roadblocks. Collaboration with peers can provide you with similar guidance and advice for avoiding mistakes and getting past roadblocks. You can also help teach your peers and mentors, and in turn become more confident in your own skills.

Working in Cybersecurity – Steps for Developing your New Cyber Career Plan ~ Gary

For our final chapter, I want to focus on building a cybersecurity career. It is my hope that as you read these paragraphs, you have been selected for the job you interviewed for, and it's time for you to do some long-term planning to develop your career roadmap. I have spoken on several occasions about how I stumbled into my career in cybersecurity. Every time I am asked to describe my process, I want to laugh; it's not like I just took a class on how to have a career in cybersecurity. It has been a lot of hard work, with many mistakes. The path I have followed has had several turns, dead ends, and restarts. This leads to the purpose of our discussion: Each person and the career course they follow will be different. Hopefully, I can provide some insight to assist you in making your path less stressful.

Know yourself

Developing a career plan is, in some ways, like trying to forecast the future. It involves planning where you want to go and determining the steps you think you need to take to get there. Before you start this process, I recommend you spend some time with yourself and with people you trust to provide you critical feedback. Now, this information you collect may not be positive, and what I mean by that is you may come to the realization you are impatient, lack some soft skills you thought you were good at, or you don't like to be around large groups of people. I bring this up because you should know your limitations; you should know those things you enjoy and those that drive you to distraction. Having this knowledge of self will help you select which roles to apply for, projects to lead, or skills to improve to grow both personally and professionally.

Conduct a skills assessment

Now that you have completed a self-assessment and understand both the limitations and advantages you bring to building a career, it's time to review your skills. There are two types of skill sets that you should check, and these are soft skills and technical (hard) skills. The technical skills you have are based on your current education and experience. It is good to document your technical skills and current knowledge level because this will also help you identify areas for improvement – hopefully, you are seeing a trend.

Now for soft skills, I am sure you are asking yourself why I would recommend you audit those as well. The reason is that for many job interviews, after you get past the first meeting with the hiring manager, you will have multiple meetings with team members and stakeholders. Honestly, the discussions will come down to whether you are a "fit" for the team. Being a "fit" for a role relies heavily on your soft skills, such as, are you a good communicator, do you work well in groups, or do you collaborate well with stakeholders?

There are numerous soft skills, and the more senior you get in your career, the more critical your soft skills become. So, I recommend you audit both your hard and soft skills to establish your career baseline, and as you progress, manage both. Having this established baseline will help you answer questions such as what soft skills do I lack for that new role? What technical skills do my mentors or peers recommend I develop if I want to work for this company? Don't forget, once you start this process, it is continuous. You should periodically review your progress to make sure you have the skills needed for your current career plan and be working on what you think you may need for future goals.

Understand the career roles available to you

The cybersecurity career field is broad and continuously changing. I state this often when I speak with people who are looking at entering the security field. I tell them that the job they start with will probably change and be something different five years from now, and this instability is typical in cybersecurity. To account for this uncertainty, it pays to understand the different types of jobs available in cyber. I would highly recommend the NICE Framework (mentioned earlier). This framework groups cybersecurity into high-level functions and documents many specialty areas within cybersecurity. Finally, this framework tries to provide a detailed description of work roles by describing the knowledge, skills, and abilities required to perform tasks within that specific role. I recommend this resource because it helps you see that there are many exciting areas where you can start your career, so get excited and select several to review.

Another resource available to help you build your career plan is Cyber Seek.[32] Cyber Seek provides an interactive map that you can use to see how cybersecurity jobs are interconnected and can provide a list of job titles, certifications, and skills required for a specific role. You can use both resources to help you build a detailed career path for where you want to go professionally and help you develop a list of skills, experience, education, and certifications you may need to acquire along the way.

Understand the dark side of this career

Now it's time to focus on the reality of working in cybersecurity. Working in this field is not how Hollywood portrays it. It is not glamorous, and all hackers don't wear hoodies. This field is a lot of hard work and stress. Working in cybersecurity is not like regular jobs because you will be on call and must be available at all hours, day or night if needed. You will find that when working in cybersecurity, there is never an end to the projects, issues, or incidents. Cybersecurity is continuous and doesn't stop.

---

[32] https://www.cyberseek.org/index.html

Also, as you may have heard, there is a massive labor shortage in this field. This means that you will typically be working in short-handed teams. Many factors are causing this shortage. Some of them are the dynamic push-pull of emerging technologies and evolving new threats. This innovation-threat cycle comes with continuous attacks by criminal syndicates on businesses, but corporations continue driving the need for new technologies and services to compete. This mix of factors really challenges and brings stress to the whole cybersecurity community.

If you plan to stay long-term in the cybersecurity field, you should plan early on managing this stress; you should develop a self-care strategy. By self-care, I mean that you should start early in your career to find things outside of cybersecurity that give you balance and purpose. This career will take all of your time and energy if you let it. It would be best to put processes in place to manage your stress, so you are here with us for the long term. Please take this seriously; I have seen stress destroy friends and cut careers short, so if you need help, ask for it.

Get involved in the community

Part of your career plan should also involve how you will give back to the cybersecurity community. If you are in this field for the long term, make it enjoyable by getting involved. In doing this, you will be able to build and expand a network of peers and friends. You will find that this community is continuously changing, and many of us are pushing for more diversity as it makes us stronger. I recommend that you include in your plan joining some professional organizations like ISC2, ISSA, or ISACA, and maybe volunteer to help at events like BSides or DefCon. What is crucial here is that for you to develop a lasting and fulfilling career in cybersecurity, you need to participate in the community; and to be honest, we need you to do that.

Continuous education

As mentioned previously, constant changes in technology and threats drive the cybersecurity industry. These drivers will also impact you and your career because cybersecurity is not a field where you will know everything. It is a field that requires you to be vigilant, and if you want to be successful, you will need to educate yourself continuously. This education may take the form of reading and writing articles, researching emerging threats and new technologies, or more formal education such as completing courses or new professional certifications. I bring this up so you can add it to your career plan.

Over my long career in information technology and cybersecurity, I added a new continuous education component to my career plan about every 18 months. Between doing courses or certifications at these career marks, I would factor in the daily reading of tech articles, blogs, podcasts, and the occasional book. Doing this will help you not only stay educated on your chosen career field but will also help you build trust with your organization's managers and leadership team. You will find that the more you know, the more you don't know <smile>, and that is normal. What is critical to remember is not to be afraid of that. Reach out to your network to ask for assistance, do research, and be willing to accept help from peers and team members. You will always be learning something new working in cybersecurity, so incorporate it into your career plan, and please share what you experience so others may grow as well.

Seek a mentor

As you begin your career, you may not have any mentors, which isn't bad. However, it will be something you will want to incorporate into your career plan as you grow professionally. Over my long career, I have had both technical (Cyber & IT) and non-technical mentors. Having mentors who were senior in my field helped me dodge some of the potholes that would have stunted my career path. Having mentors outside of cybersecurity helped provide professional clarity on issues such as how businesses are run, how to work with non-technical teams and helped me identify soft skills that I needed to focus on if I wanted to be successful. The important lesson I want you to take away from this is that having both types of mentors provides you with balance. Of course, the fun part is, where do you find them? To answer this question, it's all about getting involved in the community because mentors will not come to you. So, look for them at work, look for them at church or school, and look for them in professional organizations. One last note is to talk with your peers who are being mentored and learned how they did it. Don't forget, as you find mentors throughout your career, give back and mentor those coming behind you – it's essential to leave our community better than when you joined it.

Map your career growth

Use mind maps, post-it notes, index cards, or spreadsheets. Whatever tool you want to use doesn't matter. What is important is that you document your plan to have a visual cue that you can continuously refer to for your professional growth. My career plan is a mind map with many child boxes where I annotate research and ideas of subjects I may want to learn or technologies I find interesting. What's important is using the tools mentioned above (NICE Framework or Cyber Seek) to help create your career timeline and document your current role and any future jobs you may want to target. With this filled out, you then add existing skill sets and new ones you will need, and any certifications that may be required. Once you complete this initial career plan, it may look like a tree with different branches for you to follow, depending on the opportunities or challenges you face. Just remember, design this plan to be flexible because even with all of your hard work, there will be times you make mistakes. This uncertainty is why I recommend you periodically assess where you are on your career path and prepare yourself with continual education in case you need to pivot and change direction.

Understand business sector challenges

Different business sectors have regulations, laws, compliance requirements, and technology challenges. The longer you are in cybersecurity, the more you will have the opportunity to work in several of these sectors and find both the similarities and stark differences. I bring this topic up to think about the opportunities and challenges of specific industries and add these insights into your long-term career plan. Some industries have heavy regulatory burdens, so quick changes may not happen in those industries. If you are working in cybersecurity in one of those industries, you can expect initiatives will take longer to resource and complete, and there may be limited career growth.

Other industries may be fast-moving, with changes coming daily, and you may feel like you are continuously fighting fires. However, these fast-moving industries provide resources, you know your career is moving forward, but you also have the stress to go with your success. You can learn about the challenges and opportunities associated with these various business sectors by getting involved in the cyber community and speaking with your peers. You will find that many of us are facing challenges unique to our companies. Through speaking with peers, you can collect information on the business sectors that are right for your long-term career goals and identify those you may wish to avoid.

Collaborate, be flexible

Finally, as we finish this chapter, I want to stress a significant point… you will, over time, make mistakes and need help. Sometimes these mistakes are your fault; sometimes, you are a bystander in the process and just become part of the fallout as the business decides it needs to change. Whatever the case, you are ok because you have your career plan and a network to help you search for your next job. What I want you to understand with this final point is that your career plan should be flexible; you should have several types of roles and industries to target for your next job. It would help if you were willing to speak with peers and mentors for ideas on what you could improve. Each time in my career, when I looked for a new job, I have always approached the process as a collaborative effort. I would highly recommend you do the same, make it a community effort and be willing to not only accept help but give it to those in need as well.

Each of us travels our road during our professional careers. Sometimes this road is smooth and straight, but many times it's full of accidents and traffic jams. What is vital to remember for all of us is that we are members of a community, and even with the best career plan, it helps to have friends and peers to speak to and mentors to hold us accountable. I hope this final chapter provides the last steps you need to help you build a long and prosperous career in cybersecurity.

You Are Here, Now What? ~ Chris

One of the exciting and scary things about working in cybersecurity is that it is an industry that is continually evolving, so things are never boring, but the pace of change can be overwhelming for some people. I find myself learning new things daily about different aspects of the industry. Since cybersecurity touches everything from governance to identity to infrastructure to best practices, professionals are often called on to learn about and be expert witnesses about these different areas. Depending on your preference, you might choose to specialize in one of these domains while having a generalized knowledge in several others, or just have a generalized knowledge in all with a solid technical depth in focus areas you enjoy. The key is to ensure that you understand your areas of general or specialist knowledge, and which areas you still have a lot more you need to learn. The following topics are things I believe you as a new cybersecurity professional should be aware of, and I will close this chapter and book with some tips to help you with your career path.

Dunning-Kruger Effect

The challenge for many professionals is, to be honest about their assessments of their strengths and weaknesses and accurately judge their current level of maturity. Some new entrants to the industry suffer from over-confidence about their ability to understand the risks involved, also known as the Dunning-Kruger Effect.[33] On the other hand, those with more experience may feel that they will never have all the knowledge they need to tackle challenging situations. This is known as Imposter Syndrome.[34] Many in this industry will very much agree with this famous saying: **"The more you know, the more you realize you don't know."** ~ Aristotle. The key in these situations to find the balance between the two.

---

[33] https://en.wikipedia.org/wiki/Dunning%E2%80%93Kruger_effect
[34] https://en.wikipedia.org/wiki/Impostor_syndrome

Imposter Syndrome

Many are amazed at the types of people who admit to imposter syndrome. Whether it's a junior analyst who finally got their first role in the industry or a seasoned CISO leading protection for a billion-dollar institution, imposter syndrome is a natural part of being in an ever-changing industry where you need to continually work to keep up. The secret is to realize that this industry relies on a foundation of core security, networking, and computing concepts. Once you master these foundational concepts, you can use them in every situation to help influence decisions and problem-solving. Realistically ensuring that you know those concepts, or are on your way to learning them, will give you the confidence that you can get through many of these tough challenges.

A concept that has helped me get through bouts of imposter syndrome myself is to remember my career is a journey and that neither I nor anyone will ever know everything. The key to being successful is to know yourself (strengths and weaknesses) and identify the resources and people in your network that can help you with a particular problem.

Continuous Learning

You will need to practice continuous learning for several reasons in this field. These reasons include keeping up with the changing industry, maintaining your competitiveness in the field, and satisfying the requirements for earning continuing education credits necessary to maintain certifications.

Ever since I was 14 years old, I wanted to continuously learn more about computers, from building them up from components to securely networking them together. Today, my career has evolved to using that foundational knowledge and additional areas of expertise, including policy, governance, psychology, and sociology. I have learned that to be the best cybersecurity professional as computers and technology have become an integral part of society, I need to know how they affect and interact with the different aspects of society. I have focused on being a generalist and understanding risk, security, cloud, and business enablement. You can choose your path, mixing and matching things you are passionate about with ways to use technology to make things better.

Choosing your continuous learning path is up to you. Some will focus on getting degrees, others on certifications, while still others will focus on self-directed projects. You get to choose the best path or combination of paths for you, and this may change over time.

My passion for continuous education has had me doing them all, with several industry certifications including CISSP, CRISC, and vendor certs, a Master of Science in Information Technology, and a Bachelor of Science in Business Administration. I also find myself reading or listening to 50 to 100 books a year, completing 20 to 30 video courses, listening to hundreds of podcasts, and attending as many conferences as I can afford.

Mentee/Mentor

Asking others for help and learning from their mistakes before I make them myself has been my strategy from the beginning. I have used books, courses, and podcasts to learn as much from others as possible. However, sometimes you face problems that seem so unique that you might not know where to look for solutions, and this is where mentors come in. Mentors are individuals to whom you can reach out and ask for advice. Typically, these are more seasoned individuals than yourself and they can provide you with objective, non-emotional guidance for your situation. There is this myth that you can only have one mentor, but this is not true. You can have many mentors throughout your life, and there are many reasons for this.

Some mentors might be professional mentors who help you with detailed career advice; perhaps they are in your dream role, and you want them to share tips and guidance on what you need to do to prepare yourself for that role. Another might be a technical mentor who helps you with a specific technical challenge in your life, like preparing for a larger technical project or certification. You might also need mentors for different areas of your personal life, from health to stress management, as taking a holistic approach to your life will lead to long-term success overall. I believe it is healthy to have multiple mentors for both your personal and professional life. Mentors help you remain balanced, which is important for a long career.

Helping others helps you in return

While getting help from others is excellent, do not shy away from mentoring others too. Believe it or not, you are likely to have the skills, competencies, and experiences to help others. It is incredible how much you learn about yourself and grow while helping others. Assisting others forces you to contemplate your own experiences and try to pull advice from those experiences to help your mentees, but in that process, you are also teaching yourself.

Asking those in your network for help is beneficial for two reasons: building bonds with them and getting the assistance you might need at the time. It is essential, though, to be reciprocal in assisting them in return. By helping others, you help build your skills and competencies at the same time – this mutually beneficial relationship of helping and being helped shows how those who give also receive.

This concept has been a core component of my career. I have been fortunate enough to get a considerable amount of help from peers, mentors, and other professionals in the community. They provided me with guidance regarding areas to focus on and resources to continue my education, and provided troubleshooting guidance and other advice along the way. These individuals have helped motivate me, guide me, and show me what it takes to be a servant leader, and I pledged to myself that I would do the same for others.

Helping others is one reason my co-host (Renee Small, also a co-author of this book) and I host the podcast *Breaking into Cybersecurity*. We interview guests who have broken into the cybersecurity field in various types of roles within the past five years. They share their experiences, tips, and tricks for breaking into cybersecurity with the listeners. Renee and I continually fielded these types of questions from individuals trying to break into the field, so we thought we would scale our efforts to educate would-be cyber professionals by recording the sessions and helping anyone who wanted to listen. The podcast has grown to include senior security professionals sharing what they look for when hiring, and tackling security topics of concern from our listeners, in hopes of helping our listeners find their way.

Similarly, this book has been a labor of love trying to extract my experiences to help those looking for additional tips and tricks to find their way into this industry.

Sending the ladder back down

If you have gotten this far in this book, I hope you have already started implementing the advice given and begun to see some budding results. Continue to grow, practice your skills, and help others whenever possible. One way you can create an extraordinary impact for others is "sending the ladder back down,"[35] which is the concept of helping those who are just starting or are in an earlier stage of their career. You can assist these individuals by sharing how you grew in your career to help them grow in their own. Putting this concept into action could be as simple as introducing a hiring manager, sharing resources to advance someone's knowledge, or mentoring them through their careers.

---

[35] Please see https://www.siliconrepublic.com/companies/women-invent-100-2018-workplace for an article describing the concept of sending the ladder back down.

So, I challenge you to *send the ladder back down* and help others achieve the same success you have achieved and encourage them to do the same when they continue to grow. My goal for this is to cause a ripple effect of people helping each other and making this a more inclusive community.

Focusing on mental health to prevent "burnout"

As data becomes the most critical asset to a company's success, there is increased demand for information security professionals to secure the people, processes, and technology that make up the data-sharing ecosystem. The landscape in which companies are operating is rapidly evolving across multiple vectors, including cyber threat actors and government regulations, among others. This dynamic often requires cybersecurity professionals who can wear many hats, including operational security, compliance, and incident response. While each of these can be a role itself, many companies, especially Small-Medium-Businesses (SMBs) who might not have the budgets of larger enterprises, often expect candidates to do them all. In addition to being the jack of all cyber trades, companies expect cybersecurity professionals to be on call and respond to incidents 24/7/365. These expectations often make cybersecurity professionals feel like they need to be always on and saddles them with worry about their companies navigating the changing cyber landscape.

You need to be mindful of all the stressors associated with these types of roles and actively work to minimize or mitigate these impacts on your mental health and physical health.

Here are a couple of helpful things that can help minimize the mental health impacts of these roles on you.

Separate work from life

While cybersecurity professionals are often required to be on call, they should strive to separate their work from their home life to minimize the impact on their mental health. Many cybersecurity professionals have the luxury of working remotely, but this can often lead to a blending of work and personal time. Having a defined space can allow you to mentally separate work from home and step away from job stresses. This can be in the form of a home office or even carving out a piece of the living room. While it might be comfortable working from the couch, give your mind the chance to separate work from relaxation by maintaining separation between workspace and living space. Another way to give your mind this separation is to have hobbies that are drastically different from cybersecurity. I know people in the industry who are passionate about playing video or board games, cooking, hiking, traveling, working on cars or motorcycles, and woodworking. If you have a family, you want to ensure that you also carve out time to spend with them. Families of cybersecurity professionals often sacrifice family time and put off planning for vacations because of on-call requirements for rapid response. They know that you might get called for an incident and would need to drop whatever you are doing to respond. You want to ensure that you can carve out quality time for them.

Time for self-care

While it might be stressful being on call, there are things that you can do to prevent burnout. Taking regular breaks from work is critical to give yourself some time to breathe or stretch your muscles. I recommend taking at least five minutes an hour to take a break, which can be as simple as meditating in your chair for five minutes or taking a short walk to clear your mind. Having these types of breaks can bring clarity to ongoing situations and help you become more productive in the long run. Meditation can be as simple as a breathing exercise to clear your mind. Other examples could include journaling to help move your thoughts from your mind to paper or talking to others about your stressors to release them from your mind. Vacations are another way to help take care of yourself and step away from the job. These can be things like mini-vacations in which you turn off your phones/computers and don't think about or focus on work, or taking several days off to spend time with your family, travel to a new place, or just do nothing at home. The key to this downtime is to step away from electronic devices and focus on the present.

Congratulations! You Made It! Now What? ~ Renee

Congratulations! You made it! You're in your first cyber job. You should be very proud of yourself for staying the course and breaking into the field. This culminates all the hard work it took for you to get through all the roadblocks to get your first role in cyber. Now what?

Find a mentor (or two)

Since you've been networking through social media, professional organizations, and conferences, you may have come across some people in the field whom you look up to. Preferably these are people who have the experience that you would like to gain in the future. Reach out to one of these people and share that you admire their work and ask if they would be willing to mentor you. If they have the capacity, many people would be willing to do so. Please note that a mentor doesn't have to be years and years ahead of you. They can be where you would like to be in a few years.

Mentorship is one of the quickest ways for you to get where you aspire to be, as the mentor is willing to share their wisdom and the mistakes that they made along the way. A mentor can give you shortcuts and hacks for your career that you may not be aware of. Also, note that you can (and should) have multiple mentors. I've had many mentors in various aspects of my life, and some just have experience in an area that I don't. If you're trying to decide your path in security and determining which areas of security you'd like to pursue, you may want to seek out mentors in a few areas.

To be a great mentee, be prepared when meeting with your mentor. Do research in advance and come prepared with very specific questions. Remember that the mentor's time is very valuable, and you will need to maximize the time you share with them. Also, be prepared with what you can offer as a mentee. Mentors want to learn from their mentees as well. Maybe you have social media expertise that they don't, or you see a solution to an industry challenge that they may not be thinking about. Ask them how you can help them. You may be surprised at what your mentor needs help with, and what you can offer them.

Certifications

In almost every single conversation about security, the "which certification should I get?" question comes up. Now that you're in your first role, you can look out on the horizon to see which certifications align with your current job as well as your future roles. Your manager will be able to steer you in the right direction for the current role, and your mentor will be able to guide you for both current and future roles.

One insight that I've gained from leaders is that they pay attention to certifications that align with their current and future projects. If they have an upcoming cloud migration project and the leader needs someone who understands security in the cloud. They may look for people who have that specific cloud cert as this aligns with their project. So, reverse engineer your certs by looking out a few years to see what's coming and whether it aligns with your career goals.

Continuous Learning and Staying Current

As you are aware, nothing in technology stands still. Continuous learning and staying current with industry trends are absolute necessities in this space. Along with continuing education and attaining certifications, staying up on industry news is key in ensuring that you have the most up-to-date information in cyber.

As I have shared, the first step is to learn from your manager about upcoming projects so that you can be prepared. Maybe you ask to view the strategic plan so you can gain some sense of new technologies that may be coming to you and your team. This is where you should focus efforts on certifications and immediate education. Your management may have a plan for you, but you can be proactive and complete the education and certifications in advance. Realize that there is almost always a free version of education for whatever you need to learn in cybersecurity. If you do need the certification for your job, your employer will likely pay for it or reimburse you for it after you pass it.

If you would like to go the route of formal education and pursue a bachelor's, master's, or doctoral degree, there are numerous inexpensive options. Do your research to determine the best option based on your top criteria. If your goal is to use your additional degree for career advancement into a new opportunity, research the places that the degree program's graduates have worked after graduation. Also, research how long it took graduates to find an opportunity in their career field of choice.

You must stay updated on current events in security. Things change and move so quickly when it comes to security. There are numerous daily briefings that provide quick updates of the news that's happening regarding security, including vulnerabilities, security breaches, incidents, regulations, and more. I share a list of a few resources that you might find helpful below. However, this is a small sampling of news sources, so research and talk to colleagues about where they get news related to cybersecurity in your industry.

After you have a few years of experience under your belt and become a subject matter expert (SME) in your current area of expertise, consider expanding your skills to another area of security. This will help you to continue to grow in the field and help with diversifying your skills and new roles you could pursue. With updated and relevant skillsets, you will continue to be ahead of the curve when it comes to securing newer technologies. You will also become a magnet for hiring leaders who look for people with bleeding-edge experience.

Resources

- List of 48 Cybersecurity podcasts. This list is not exhaustive but a great starting point for podcasts.
  https://www.frontlines.io/top-cybersecurity-podcasts
- List of 45 Cybersecurity news sites.
  https://blog.feedspot.com/cyber_security_news_websites/

Chapter 11 – Key Points and Recommended Actions

- Getting your first job in cybersecurity is not the finish line, it's the starting line. Now that you are here, we welcome you, and suggest you immediately begin to update your career plan. Begin with a self-assessment to catalog your strengths and your areas for growth with the new lens of advancing your cybersecurity career rather than getting your first cybersecurity job.
- Key to your self-assessment and your career plan are healthy relationships with mentors and mentees. Continue to build your human network, adding people in your new profession you can learn from. And be generous in helping others trying to make a change or grow. Not only is it good karma to give back, but we learn about ourselves when we try to articulate our thoughts and values to others.
- As Gary said, this field is constantly evolving, if for no other reason than companies will never stop innovating in their product lines and bad actors will never stop devising new ways to attack. Therefore, you must be in continuous learning mode. But don't just learn enough to tread water, push your envelope and grow. Stay curious!
- Because of the constant battle that defines cybersecurity, you will be under constant pressure. Self-care is an essential part of your career plan. While everyone will recognize the need for self-care, rarely will others put your self-care first. You will need to have a plan and advocate for your needs. Burnout is a very real danger in this field.
- Connect with your new community. Join professional groups, join informal discussion groups, read, listen to podcasts, engage, ask questions, answer questions. More than any other field we've witnessed, this field is all about community. Get involved and stay involved.

Conclusion

We chose not to end this book after you went on your interview, but with advice about how to build upon your successful job search. As we said in the introduction, "For those that want to explore a career in cybersecurity, we first want to say, 'Welcome, we need the help!'"

Throughout *Develop Your Cybersecurity Career Path*, we have shared our perspectives about the career, the community, and the commitment evident in our chosen career field. It's no accident that the word "community" is the most often used word in this book. We even defined the term in the introduction to Chapter 5. By now, it is probably obvious that we believe the path to a career in cybersecurity is made less arduous by embracing our community of like-minded cybersecurity professionals.

Now that you have completed this book, you should have a better idea of your passions, your skills, your connections, and the mechanics of breaking into cybersecurity. We wish you well!

We welcome your feedback and invite you to visit our website: http://www.cisodrg.com or our LinkedIn company page: https://www.linkedin.com/company/ciso-desk-reference-guide.

About the Authors

With over 20 years of IT, Cybersecurity, and Risk Management experience, Gary Hayslip has established a reputation as a highly skilled communicator, author, and keynote speaker. Currently, as Chief Information Security Officer for Softbank Investment Advisers (SBIA), he advises executive leadership on protecting critical information resources and overseeing enterprise cybersecurity strategy. Hayslip recently co-authored the *CISO Desk Reference Guide: A Practical Guide for CISOs – Volumes 1 and 2*, which enable CISOs to expand their business and leadership expertise. Hayslip also recently published *The Essential Guide to Cybersecurity for SMBs*, a practical guidebook for the SMB security professional. Hayslip's previous executive experience includes multiple CISO, CIO, Deputy Director of IT and Chief Privacy Officer roles for the U.S. Navy (Active Duty), the U.S. Navy (Federal Government employee), the City of San Diego California, and Webroot Software.

LinkedIn: https://www.linkedin.com/in/ghayslip/
CISO Desk Reference Website: https://cisodrg.com/

Christophe Foulon focuses on helping to secure people and process with a solid understanding of the technology involved. He has over 10 years of experience as an Information Security Manager and Cybersecurity Strategist with a passion for customer service, process improvement, and information security. He has significant experience in optimizing the use of technology, while balancing the implications to people, process, and information security by using a consultative approach.

LinkedIn: www.linkedin.com/in/christophefoulon
cpfcoaching.wordpress.com

Renee Small is the CEO of Cyber Human Capital, one of the leading human resources business partners in the field of cyber security, and author of the Amazon #1 best-selling book, *Magnetic Hiring: Your Company's Secret Weapon to Attracting Top Cyber Security Talent.* She is committed to helping leaders close the cybersecurity talent gap by hiring from within and helping more people get into the lucrative cyber security profession.

LinkedIn Profile: https://www.linkedin.com/in/reneebrownsmall/
Magnetic hiring: https://www.amazon.com/dp/1521783446/

Made in the USA
Las Vegas, NV
15 February 2024

85823523R00164